Measuring National POWER in the Postindustrial Age

Ashley J. Tellis • Janice Bially • Christopher Layne • Melissa McPherson

Prepared for the United States Army

RAND | Arroyo Center

For more information on the RAND Arroyo Center, contact the Director of Operations, (310) 393-0411, extension 6500, or visit the Arroyo Center's Web site at http://www.rand.org/organization/ard/

PREFACE

The arrival of postindustrial society has given rise to the suspicion that the traditional bases of national power have been fundamentally transformed and, as such, that the indices used to measure the relative power of nations should be reassessed as well. This suspicion has special resonance given the fact that countries like the Soviet Union and Iraq, classified as relatively significant powers by some aggregate indicators of capability, either collapsed through internal enervation or proved utterly ineffectual when their capabilities were put to the test in war. Both these examples suggest that appreciating the true basis of national power requires not merely a meticulous detailing of visible military assets but also a scrutiny of larger capabilities embodied in such variables as the aptitude for innovation, the nature of social institutions, and the quality of the knowledge base—all of which may bear upon a country's capacity to produce the one element that is still fundamental to international politics: effective military power. To the degree that contemporary intelligence approaches fail to integrate information of this sort, they may be deficient insofar as visible military indicators will provide important—but still incomplete and perhaps misleading—assessments of "true" national power.

This report represents a "first cut" at reconfiguring the notion of national power to accommodate a wider understanding of capability than is now used in discussions about international affairs. The intention here is to advance a conceptual framework that helps the intelligence community develop better evaluative measures of the national capabilities of countries likely to become potential peer competitors of the United States. This framework, insofar as it captures a more comprehensive view of national power that helps distinguish “truly” powerful from “apparently” powerful countries, is intended to support the Army’s and the intelligence community’s efforts at long-range planning and global forecasting. These efforts obviously seek to assess the capabilities of potential adversaries as accurately as possible in order to meter appropriate military acquisitions, structures, and development on the part of the United States.

The research reported in this document was sponsored by the Deputy Chief of Staff for Intelligence and was conducted in the Strategy, Doctrine, and Resources Program of RAND’s Arroyo Center, a federally funded research and development center sponsored by the United States Army.

CONTENTS

FIGURES

SUMMARY

The arrival of postindustrial society has given rise to the suspicion that the traditional bases of national power have changed; if this is so, the indices used to measure the relative power of nations should be reassessed as well. This suspicion has special resonance given the fact that countries like the Soviet Union and Iraq, classified as relatively significant powers by some aggregate indicators of capability, either collapsed through internal enervation or proved utterly ineffectual when their capabilities were put to the test in war. Both these examples suggest that appreciating the true basis of national power requires not merely a meticulous detailing of visible military assets but also a scrutiny of larger capabilities embodied in such variables as the aptitude for innovation, the nature of social institutions, and the quality of the knowledge base—all of which conceivably bear upon a country's capacity to produce the one element that is still fundamental to international politics: effective military power. To the degree that contemporary intelligence approaches lack information of this sort, they may be deficient insofar as the emphasis on gross indicators provides important—but still incomplete and perhaps misleading—assessments of true national power.

This report represents a "first cut" at reconfiguring the notion of national power to accommodate a wider understanding of capability than is currently utilized in discussions about international affairs. The intention here is to develop a conceptual framework that provides better evaluative measures of the national capabilities of countries likely to become potential peer competitors of the United States. Toward that end, the framework offered in this report integrates some existing measures of national power like size of population, GNP, and the capabilities of the armed forces with other, newer measures of capability flowing from a detailed reassessment of the nature of the "state" itself. Unlike most traditional approaches to power measurement—which treat countries as "bordered resource containers" with measurable attributes of the sort identified above—the framework offered in this report unpacks the concept of "country" in order to look *within* what was previously treated as a black box.

Unpacking the concept of country enables national entities to be viewed as active social structures rather than as mere geographical containers, and it allows national power to be seen as produced by three distinct realms, every one of which is as important as the other for the generation of usable power in international politics. The first realm encompasses the level of resources either available to or produced by a country; the second realm encompasses national performance deriving both from the external pressures facing a country and the efficiency of its governing institutions, nominally labeled the "state," and its society at large; and, finally, the third realm encompasses military capability, which is understood in terms of operational proficiency or effectiveness produced as a result of both the strategic resources available to a military organization and its ability to convert those resources into effective coercive power. These three realms taken together describe national power. The analysis offered in this report elaborates the rationale for assessing each of these components as well as proffers ideas on how they might be measured in tangible ways.

Because of the great detail inherent in the analysis, this framework is not intended for cross-national comparisons on a large scale. Rather, it is more appropriate for the close scrutiny of a few significant powers in the international system, one at a time. In any event, the analytical framework offered here is not intended to be a complete statement of intelligence-collection requirements. The data sought may not be collected by the intelligence community, and in some cases may simply be too complicated or too difficult to collect. Even if all these data were available, however, this framework will not allow any "automatic computation" of a given country's national power. Any framework that enables such computation would of necessity be sparse and parsimonious. By virtue of this fact, it would also not provide the detailed "national power profile" that the intelligence community needs to make critical judgments about whether certain candidate great powers are on the cusp of becoming true peer competitors of the United States.

Since this framework is fundamentally oriented toward assisting the intelligence community in its efforts to create a standardized power profile of such candidate great powers, it must—almost by definition—be sufficiently detailed while still reserving room for the specialized knowledge that country specialists and regional analysts will invariably bring to bear in the production of any strategic assessments. The purpose of this framework, in the first instance, is therefore heuristic: it is meant to identify what a comprehensive understanding of national power requires in the postindustrial age and, to that degree, is intended to contribute to the discussions now taking place within the intelligence community about what the appropriate measures of national power ought to be. In the final instance, however, it is intended to supply an intellectual "template" which, if found suitable and after further modification, the intelligence community could use to define future collection requirements for purposes of constructing power profiles of certain key countries of interest to the United States.

Three distinct premises undergird the analytic framework offered in this report. The first premise is that something resembling a science-based "knowledge revolution," most clearly manifested by the current breakthroughs in information processing, technology, and management, is currently under way in society at large and that this phenomenon has consequential effects in both the civilian and the military realm. The second premise is that the performance of the "state," understood precisely as the governing institutions that steer a nation's political direction, will be critical to a country's success in the postindustrial age because no matter how successful a given society may be in developing or exploiting the science-based knowledge revolution currently taking place, a minimally efficient state is required if these societal advances are to be transformed into national power. The third premise is that national power will continue to be expressed—ultimately—in terms of warfighting capabilities and that the most important kind of warfighting capabilities are those that exploit critical emerging technologies, especially those relating to information and communications technologies, to produce militarily effective conventional forces.

Taken together, these premises imply that the framework for analyzing national power advanced in this report—and depicted below in graphic form—focuses on assessing what a given country must possess if it is to effectively create and utilize the emerging technological changes to produce those capabilities that will ultimately advantage it in the arena of international politics.

As mentioned above, the framework offered here for assessing national power divides the polity into three distinct realms. The first realm seeks to depict the national resources a country must possess if it is to develop capabilities that enable it to produce an effective military force. Since the beginning of the modern international system, these capabilities have usually been measured by variables such as population, size of territory, economic strength (usually measured in terms of GNP/GDP), and natural resources. Since these measures cannot simply be jettisoned, we incorporated them in our framework in the context of other, newer qualitative variables that speak to a country's wider ability to incorporate the science-based knowledge revolution in their political, economic, and social spheres. This ability to incorporate the knowledge revolution in every realm of material life is critical because the changes in the political, economic, and social spheres are themselves seen as creating the foundations for new forms of military power. The inputs of national power identified

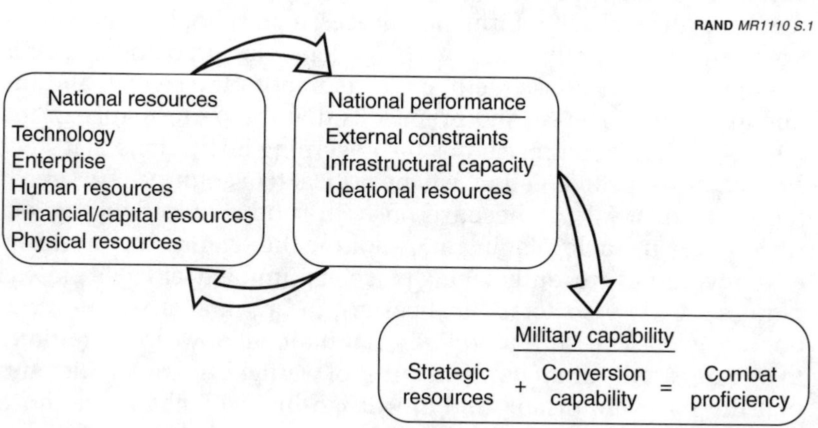

Figure S.1—A Revised View of National Power

in this framework are discussed here under the rubric of (1) technology, (2) enterprise, (3) human resources, (4) financial/capital resources, and (5) physical resources.

The second realm seeks to capture the mechanisms that enable countries to create or convert national resources, which represent latent power, into tangible forms of usable power. The objective of introducing this "transformative" dimension of national power is to move beyond the traditional view of countries as "bordered power-containers" to something that models countries as active social structures consisting of state and societal actors and institutions, all of which exist in an environment populated by many similar entities abroad. Introducing this dimension allows the framework to capture an element that most traditional measures of power cannot accommodate: a state's relationship to both its external environment and its own society and the consequences thereof for national power capability. In particular, this level of analysis allows the observer to assess the levels of external pressures confronting a given country as well as how aware and responsive a particular state-society complex is to the new resources that must be produced if the country is to develop the effective military capabilities referred to earlier. In this realm, the three variables examined are (1) the external constraints emerging from the international system, (2) the infrastructural capacity of a given state, and (3) its ideational resources.

The third realm seeks to capture the tangible military capability produced by a country. Military capabilities are considered to be the effective manifestation of national power because they represent the projectible power that a country can bring to bear against other competitors which, in the anarchic system of international politics, constitutes its first line of defense. Military capabilities in this framework are understood to be a resultant product of the continual, cyclic *interaction* of both national resources and national performance: resources may be "building blocks," but these building blocks, far from existing in nature, must be consciously produced as a result of human artifice, which is captured, however imperfectly, by the domain of national performance. The institutions inhabiting this latter realm, in turn, rely on the resources they have produced both to maintain themselves internally and to expand their own (or their country's) power externally, and the most important manifestation of this external power is military capability. Many traditional indexes of national power have incorporated military capabilities in some form or another, though this was usually done through the use of summary variables such as level of military expenditure or gross size of the armed forces. In its focus on military capabilities, our framework seeks a greater level of detail. The examination of military capability is patterned like the larger framework for assessing national power. It identifies (1) the strategic resources a military receives from the government it serves, which include defense budgets, manpower, military infrastructure, combat RDT&E institutions, the defense industrial base, and the warfighting inventory and support; (2) the variables bearing upon how these resources are converted into effective capabilities, such as the threats facing a country and the strategy developed to cope with them; the structure of civil-military relations; the density of foreign military-to-military relations; the nature of doctrine, training, and organization; and the potential and capacity for innovation; and (3) the capabilities of the combat force itself, understood via a spectrum of warfighting competencies which may be attained to a greater or lesser degree and which may be compared across countries.

Chapter One

INTRODUCTION: WHY THE INTEREST IN NATIONAL POWER?

THE EMERGING INFORMATION TECHNOLOGY REVOLUTION

It is widely argued today that human societies are in the process of a momentous transition. Nearly three centuries into the industrial era—an era distinguished by, among other things, the dramatic substitution of mechanical for animal power and the ubiquitous presence of mass production—it is now believed that society stands on the threshold of a new age defined fundamentally by the presence of a science-based knowledge revolution. This idea, however, is by no means novel. As early as 1973, Daniel Bell, in a pathbreaking study titled *The Coming of Post Industrial Society: A Venture in Social Forecasting,* argued that there would soon emerge a society "organized around knowledge for the purpose of social control and the directing of innovation and change."[1] This idea, however, acquired a new lease on life, at least in the popular imagination, when the authors Alvin and Heidi Toffler asserted that the new microelectronics, data processing, data storage, and communications technologies now visible everywhere constitute nothing less than a "third wave" in the evolution of civilization.[2] This "wave," like the agricultural and industrial waves before it, is viewed as rooted essentially in the radical changes taking place in what Marx called "the mode of

---

[1]Daniel Bell, *The Coming of Post Industrial Society: A Venture in Social Forecasting* (New York: Basic Books, 1973), p. 20.

[2]Alvin and Heidi Toffler, *War and Anti-War: Survival at the Dawn of the 21st Century* (Boston: Little, Brown and Company, 1993), pp. 18–25.

production in material life."[3] These changes derive as much from innovations in science and technology as they do from the pattern of economic relations within society: insofar as they are instantiated in the "information technology revolution," they constitute a maturing of the "age of automation,"[4] in which the combined computational and communicative power of networked computers promises to alter traditional organizational forms as well as the distribution of power within and among societies.

The emerging information technology revolution is, in the view of its proponents, both novel and significant. To be sure, the modern antecedents of these technologies go back to the 19th century, when the telegraph, the undersea cable, and the telephone first made their appearance and heralded a consequential transformation in military capability.[5] They continued to mature through the invention of radio, television, and computers in the first half of the 20th century and acquired systemically revolutionary properties since the 1950s, when solid-state electronics and the silicon chip—together with all the innovations in microelectronics that these examples have come to represent—combined to set apart the last forty-odd years from all prior history. As one analysis summarized this dynamic,

> since the 1950s, the means for communicating, processing, accessing, storing, managing, and exploiting information have exploded. No dimension of human affairs, including population or depredation of the environment, seems to have grown or changed so rapidly. In the past decade alone, measurement of the information revolution on almost any dimension—numbers (of telephone circuits, television receivers, videocassette recorders, video cameras, or facsimile machines), capacities (of transmission media, storage devices, or displays), speed, or cost—is described not in mere percentages, but in factors of three, ten or more.[6]

---

[3]Karl Marx, *A Contribution to the Critique of Political Economy,* 2d rev. ed. (New York: The International Library Publishing Co., 1904), p. 3.

[4]Martin van Creveld, *Technology and War* (New York: Free Press, 1989), p. 235ff.

[5]Peter G. Hall and Paschal Preston, *The Carrier Wave* (Boston: Unwin & Hyman, 1988).

[6]Steve Bankes and Carl Builder, *Seizing the Moment: Harnessing the Information Technologies* (Santa Monica, CA: RAND, N-3336-RC, 1992), p. 3.

The novelty of such change would be merely interesting were it not for the dramatic economic and political significance attributed to it. The Tofflers, for example, elaborating on their grand metaphor of a "third wave," assert that information technologies will in fact denature the industrial age insofar as information processing regimes will replace manufacturing as a source of wealth and growth. In this world view, now widely accepted throughout the United States, services will supplant manufacturing, hierarchic social structures will be replaced by "flat" or "networked" organizations, and in general the emphasis on "mass" production witnessed throughout the industrial era will be replaced by an emphasis on "customized" manufacturing, where efficiency is measured by the ability to satisfy multiple sets of smaller but more discriminating consumers.[7]

More pertinently, however, these changes in the "the mode of production in material life" are seen to presage a military revolution as well. As the Tofflers' popular work *War and Anti-War* succinctly argues, "this remarkable change in the world economy is bringing with it a parallel revolution in the nature of warfare,"[8] since "the way we make war reflects the way we make wealth."[9] Thus, the changes in the system of producing wealth *inevitably* will bring in their trail "revolution[s] in the system for making war . . . ,"[10] a hypothesis that seems to find considerable favor in the burgeoning literature on the "revolution in military affairs."[11] The expectations about this revolution's implications for future warfare obviously run very high insofar as the new information technologies are seen as seeking not simply "to reduce the chance and uncertainty in war"[12] but actually to replace "Caesar's augury, Montecuccoli's blend of science and mys-

---

[7]These phenomena are usefully summarized in Brian Nichiporuk and Carl H. Builder, *Information Technologies and the Future of Land Warfare* (Santa Monica, CA: RAND, MR-560-A, 1995), pp. 25–45.

[8]Toffler, op. cit., p. 5.

[9]Ibid., p. 3.

[10]Ibid., p. 35.

[11]See, by way of example, Paul Bracken, "The Military After Next," *The Washington Quarterly,* Vol. 16, No. 4 (Autumn 1993), pp. 157–174; Antulio J. Echevarria and John M. Shaw, "The New Military Revolution: Post Industrial Change," *Parameters* (Winter 1992–93), pp. 70–77; and Eliot Cohen, "A Revolution in Warfare," *Foreign Affairs,* Vol. 75, No. 2 (1996), pp. 37–54.

[12]Echevarria and Shaw, op. cit., p. 75.

ticism, Von Bulow's enlightenment formulas, Clausewitz's *coup d'oeil,* and Von Mellenthin's *Fingerspitzengefuhl.*"[13]

Whether the new information technologies can actually fulfill these lofty expectations only time will tell, but in the meantime, it is possible to speculate that they might have three more clearly discernible effects. At one level, the revolutionary consequences for warfare brought about by emerging information technologies may materialize simply at a military-technical level in that information technologies could replace the current "dumb" weapons and traditional forms of military organization with alternatives that alter the "fundamental relationship between offense and defense, space and time, [and] fire and maneuver."[14] At another level, they may lead to new socially relevant forms of warfare such as "information attacks" on infrastructures like electric power, air traffic, financial links, and oil and gas networks that result in systematic neutralization of many critical grids without any physical destruction, at least in the first instance.[15]

At a far more fundamental level, however, emerging information technology could, it is often argued, lead to a restructuring of the political order itself, both within countries and between states.[16] Such an outcome would be far more revolutionary than either of the two lower-order consequences identified above. In fact, some already see the epochal political revolutions in Eastern Europe during the 1989–1991 period "as the dramatic debut of a new era in which the sources of power and the nature of conflict are undergoing

---

[13]Ibid.

[14]Cohen, op. cit., p. 44. See also Dan Goure, "Is There a Military-Technical Revolution in America's Future?" *The Washington Quarterly,* Vol. 16, No. 4 (1993), pp. 175–192. For excellent surveys of how information technologies are altering opportunities for U.S. military power, see Edward Harshberger and David Ochmanek, "Information and Warfare: New Opportunities for U.S. Military Forces," and Brian Nichiporuk, "U.S. Military Opportunities: Information-Warfare Concepts of Operation," in Zalmay M. Khalilzad and John White (eds.), *The Changing Role of Information in Warfare* (Santa Monica, CA: RAND, 1999), pp. 157–178, 179–215.

[15]Roger C. Molander et al., *Strategic Information Warfare: A New Face of War* (Santa Monica, CA: RAND, MR-661-OSD, 1996).

[16]A fascinating exploration of how the information technology revolution may impact the forms of political order can be found in David Ronfeldt, *Tribes, Institutions, Markets, Networks: A Framework About Societal Evolution* (Santa Monica, CA: RAND, P-7967, 1996).

a fundamental shift because of the networking and shrinking of the world due to the enormous increases in the flow of information."[17] If such a conception of what information technologies can achieve is true, it would not be surprising to conclude, as one thoughtful survey did, that "it seems not improbable that the power of information, in the hands of individuals, will come to be seen as a rival to that of the nation-state; that information can be used effectively to prevent war or to wage it; and that information can be exploited to perfect or destroy entire societies."[18]

UNDERSTANDING NATIONAL POWER IN THE POSTINDUSTRIAL AGE

It is against a backdrop of such considerations that the Office of Deputy Chief of Staff for Intelligence (ODCSINT), U.S. Army, tasked RAND's Arroyo Center to undertake a conceptual examination of how national power ought to be understood in the context of the technical and social changes taking place today. There was clearly a sense that new technologies, including those in the information arena and elsewhere, had generated nontrivial changes in the traditional bases of power and, as such, warranted a review of the extant conceptions of national power as well as the customary indices used to measure the power of countries. Three concerns in particular made such a reassessment particularly pressing.

First, there has been a growing unease with the current aggregate measures of national power used within the intelligence community and to some extent within the academic community as well. These measures, which focus largely on discrete variables like size of population, GNP, size of the armed forces, extent of land area, access to exploitable resources, and annual grain and steel production, all taken together provide a rough picture of gross national power that, however interesting and useful, still fails to capture critical details about a given country's capabilities in international politics.

Second, there has been a growing suspicion that the nature of warfare itself may be changing in fundamental ways. These changes

---

[17]Bankes and Builder, op. cit., p. 3.

[18]Ibid., p. 4.

might in fact be occurring not simply at the interstate end of the conflict spectrum, as the "revolution in military affairs" theorists invariably point out, but also at the lower end of the spectrum. The changes here appear to materialize in the form of a resurgence in substatal conflicts and intrastate violence that often do not involve conventional military operations in the traditional sense. Thus, it appears quite unclear whether and, if so, how the traditional measures of national power are affected by such changes in the character of warfare.

Third, there has been increasing concern that the lack of an adequate methodology to assess national power might cause the United States to miss or misinterpret incipient changes in power capability that may be taking place within many countries in the international system. This concern is clearly fundamental: it is rooted in a legitimate fear that the absence of a good metric for judging national capabilities might result in an intelligence failure that provokes either an inappropriate overreaction or underreaction—both of which could be problematic in different ways—on the part of the United States vis-à-vis other competing entities.

These three concerns acquire special resonance given the fact that countries like the Soviet Union and Iraq, which were classified as relatively significant powers by some aggregate indicators of capability, ultimately either collapsed through internal enervation or proved to be utterly ineffectual when their capabilities were put to the test in war. Both these examples suggest that appreciating the true basis of national power may require not merely a meticulous detailing of tangible military assets such as force inventories and logistics capabilities, but also an assessment of other intangible elements like training, doctrine, leadership, experience, readiness, and integrative skill. Even more importantly, however, it seems to suggest that standard measures of power like GNP and annual economic growth rates ought to be placed within a larger scrutiny that addresses issues like the external environment facing a country as well as the aptitude of its populace for innovation, the nature of its domestic economic and social institutions, the constitution of its state-society relations, the quality of its knowledge base, and the character of its ideational ethos—all of which conceivably bear upon a country's capacity to produce the one element that is still fundamental to international politics: effective military power. To the degree that contemporary intelligence methodologies lack information of this sort, they risk being shown up as deficient since gross or aggregate national indicators will provide important, but nonetheless incomplete and perhaps misleading, assessments of "true" national power.

This report represents a first cut at reconfiguring the notion of national power to accommodate a wider understanding of capability than is currently utilized in discussions about international affairs. It is by no means complete as an intellectual product, but it is nonetheless offered in the hope that it might be improved by the criticism of others or further developed by those with an interest in this subject. The principal intention here is to develop a conceptual framework for thinking about national power in the postindustrial age, a framework directed ultimately toward helping the intelligence community advance better *evaluative* measures for a country's power capability. These measures are intended to inform the intelligence community's judgment about the national capabilities of a few candidate great powers that could become true "peer competitors" of the United States at some point in the future: far from functioning as a scoring system that eliminates judgment, they are designed to incorporate and systematize the knowledge of country and regional analysts into a template that provides detailed information on national capacity that can then be compared across a small group of peers. This objective implies that the measures alluded to, or suggested, in this report will include both hard and soft factors, both traditional and nontraditional indices. The high level of detail is designed to capture the most important dimensions of a nation's power, some of them derived from permanently relevant variables and others rooted in more novel factors that have acquired importance thanks to the peculiarities of the postindustrial age. Because of this detail, the overall framework is *not* intended to be used for cross-national comparisons on a large scale, but only for the close scrutiny of a few significant target states—one at a time.

The framework is intentionally not designed to provide "automatic" numerical scores about a country's power capacity. Rather, it is advanced primarily to order a way of thinking about national power and thus is no substitute for the knowledge and judgment of various country specialists. With more work, it could certainly be winnowed down and further translated into the "essential elements of information" of specific interest to the intelligence community, but as it currently stands, it is not a completed matrix that defines actual collection requirements. In fact, some of the data sought by the framework are not collected by the intelligence community at all; other data are collected by academic and research institutions but need further evaluation and analysis by the intelligence community to be useful; still other data called for may simply be too complicated or too difficult to collect, but are nonetheless identified because they relate to certain elusive variables that are important for understanding national power. Even if all these data were available, however, this framework will still not allow any "automatic computation" of a country's power. Any framework that enabled such computation would of necessity be sparse and parsimonious. By virtue of this fact, it would also not generate the detailed "national power profile" that the intelligence community seeks in order to make critical judgments about whether certain "candidate great powers" are on the cusp of becoming true "peer competitors" of the United States.

Since this framework is fundamentally oriented toward helping the intelligence community create such a standardized power profile of certain key countries of interest to the United States, it must—almost by definition—be sufficiently detailed while leaving room for the specialized knowledge that country specialists and regional analysts will invariably bring to bear in the production of any strategic assessments. The purpose of this framework, in the first instance, is therefore heuristic: it is meant to identify what a comprehensive understanding of national power requires in the postindustrial age and, to that degree, is intended to contribute toward the discussions now taking place in the intelligence community about what the appropriate measures of national power ought to be. In the final instance, however, it is intended to supply an intellectual "template" that, if found suitable and after further modification, the intelligence community could use to define future collection requirements for purposes of constructing power profiles of key target countries important to the United States.

If the framework advanced in this report, therefore, succeeds either in highlighting some critical dimensions of national capability that usually tend to be overlooked or in identifying some useful nontraditional measures of power that have acquired importance in the postindustrial era, it will have served its purpose. This purpose, fundamentally, consists of being able to capture a comprehensive view of power that helps distinguish "truly" powerful from only "apparently" powerful countries in a format that can be standardized for purposes of intelligence collection and comparison across a few relevant cases. Truly powerful countries are those that: possess, and invest in producing, significant levels of resources relevant to the postindustrial age; can engage in intense political-military competition with their peers over long stretches of time because their superior state structures and high ideational acuity allows them to extract and transform societal resources efficiently and on a large scale; and can develop and field highly sophisticated military forces that are operationally competent at the most demanding operations mounted against a diverse variety of adversaries. Apparently powerful countries, in contrast, are those with large military forces: they may possess nominally sophisticated inventories of weapons, but their operational proficiency is an open question. The quality of their national resource base and their ability to efficiently extract and transform societal resources are similarly problematic, with the result that such countries often display an appearance of great capability even though the national and societal foundations of their power are quite hollow. Understanding the essence of national power, as opposed to merely the appearance of it, and capturing that essence in a standardizable format that enables data collection and comparison across a small number of candidate great powers, remain the fundamental motives beneath the development of the framework offered in this report. This research will best support the Army's and the intelligence community's efforts at long-range planning and global forecasting insofar as assessing the "true" capabilities of potential adversaries as accurately as possible is vital to adequately metering our own evolving military acquisitions, structures, and development.

THE NATURE AND CONTENT OF THIS REPORT

In developing this new framework for assessing national power, the intellectual presupposition is that the bases for generating effective power are changing in significant ways thanks to the knowledge revolution, especially as manifested today in information and other emerging technologies. This research effort, however, does not scrutinize in any detail the nature of this revolution itself or its progeny, the revolution in military affairs. There is a vast and growing literature on each of these two issues, and wading into it in order to judge the debates that concern its protagonists—Is it a "revolution" or merely an "evolution"? How deeply is the "revolution" or "evolution" entrenched? What are its consequences for society and warfare?—would have taken the project too far afield to be of any use to its sponsors. Consequently, this research effort simply presumes that significant technological transformations are under way and that their broad dimensions are sufficiently discernible in both the civilian and the military realms. We have focused primarily on assessing what a given country must have if it is to effectively use the emerging knowledge revolution to produce the capabilities that will confer advantage in the arena of international politics. This assessment is then used to discern what measures relating to national capacity the intelligence community should focus on when developing its singular and comparative assessments of power.

The new conceptual framework set forth in this report has been developed in response to one deceptively simple tasking question: "How can the nature of national power be judged in this postindustrial age?" Or, empirically stated, "How would the intelligence community know if Country *X* was evolving into an effective peer competitor of the United States?" While the answer to these questions is described conceptually by means of the framework detailed in Chapter Four, the report attempts to situate this answer within a larger reflection of the nature of power itself and in the context of previous answers provided by scholars. Chapter Two identifies the conceptual considerations that must be faced when addressing the nature of national power. It begins by examining the abstract concept of "power" and then relates those considerations to the idea of "national power." Chapter Three reviews several traditional approaches to national power found in the literature, describing what insights they sought to provide. Chapter Four provides a revised view of national power that attempts to expand on the prevailing view: specifically, it attempts to show how a more comprehensive view of national power must include not simply resources and military power of the kinds traditionally measured, but new ones as well. In particular, it argues that the crucial missing link—the transformative dimension consisting of the external environment, the infrastructural power of the state, and the ideational resources of the polity—must be restored if a seamless assessment of national capability is to be obtained. Chapters Five through Seven elaborate the revised framework for measuring national power in three distinct realms: national resources, national performance, and military capability. They provide the analytical rationale for the various components held to be significant in the production of national power and suggest numerous indicators that allow measurement of the strength of these components. These indicators are primarily illustrative, but are offered as a starting point from which the intelligence community can define the "essential elements of information" (EEIs) it needs to guide its collection and analysis requirements. When viewed in their totality, the indicators are selected both to reflect the strength of the components essential to the production of national power and to provide internal cross-checks on the various data that ought to be collected. These indicators are summarized—with minimal analytical backdrop—in a companion document, RAND report MR-1110/1-A, for the convenience of various users in the intelligence community. Chapter Eight concludes the report by recapitulating the objective and the nature of the work and identifying the tasks for future research. Since this report provides a wide variety of empirical indicators interspersed with larger analytical arguments, the Appendix provides an abbreviated list of the most important *quantitative* indicators of national power in the postindustrial age. Drawn on the assumption that the intelligence community may not be able to collect and collate the diverse pieces of information identified in the report for purely practical reasons, the short list of indicators identified in the Appendix is based on the template described in Chapter Four of the report and represents the minimally necessary quantitative information for judging national capabilities in the postindustrial age.

Chapter Two

"POWER" AND "NATIONAL POWER": SOME CONCEPTUAL CONSIDERATIONS

EXAMINING THE ABSTRACT CONCEPT OF POWER

The notion of "power" underlies most analyses of politics, yet it remains one of the most contested concepts in the social sciences. In its most general sense, power is often treated as a synonym for rule. At other times, it is assumed to be an attribute of individuals. And, very commonly today, it is used as a description of group capabilities in the context of social relations among various collectivities.[1] Numerous other conceptions of power abound: it is sometimes treated as if rooted in psychology, and at other times it is viewed as a property of the political, organizational, economic, or military realms. It is also frequently seen as being connected to the notions of influence, coercion, and control. Given this vast diversity of usage, it is tempting to conclude that there are probably as many conceptions of power as there are theorists.

Yet despite the apparently wide variety of definitions and usage, it is possible to argue that most notions of power, at least in the social sciences, finally boil down to three connected but different approaches. In their succinct analysis of the term, Raymond Boudon and Francois Bourricaud argue that these three notions of power must be made explicit if the term is to be usefully employed as a concept of analysis. In the first instance, they argue that power refers to some "*allocation of resources,* of whatever nature these might be." Secondly, it refers to the "*ability* to use these resources," implying,

[1]For an analysis of these conceptions, see Dennis H. Wrong, *Power: Its Forms, Bases, and Uses* (New Brunswick: Transaction Publishers, 1995), pp. vii–xvii.

among other things, "a plan of use" and some "minimal information about the *conditions and consequences* of this use." Finally, the notion of power refers to its "*strategic* character," which is seen in the exercise "not only against the inertia of things, but also against the *resistance of opposing wills*."[2]

This tripartite approach to power can be restated using a simple taxonomy that describes power as "resources," as "strategies," and as "outcomes."[3]

Power understood as resources essentially describes the sum total of the *capabilities* available to any entity for influencing others. Traditionally these capabilities have been treated as akin to a stock concept, at least as far as international politics is concerned; thus a long and distinguished list of scholars have used such capabilities measures as the extent of natural resources, population, the armed forces, and the gross national product of countries to rank order the standing of nations.[4] The advantage of this approach is that it allows one to rank diverse entities, be they individuals or states, in a fairly consistent manner using variables that are readily observable or measurable. The problem, however, is that it is not always clear which resources are appropriate as measures of real power, or whether the resources nominally possessed in any given instance are actually usable by the actor in question. Despite these difficulties, however, the concept of power as resources has remained attractive enough and will not be easily discarded.

Rather than focusing on capabilities in any tangible or intangible sense, the second approach to power—understood as strategies—attempts to capture the *processes, relationships, and situations* through which entities intend to influence one another. Thus, in

---

[2]All quotations in this paragraph are drawn from Raymond Boudon and Francois Bourricaud, *A Critical Dictionary of Sociology* (Chicago: University of Chicago Press, 1989), p. 267. Emphases added.

[3]A similar taxonomy can be found in Kal J. Holsti, *International Politics: A Framework for Analysis* (Englewood Cliffs: Prentice-Hall, 1983), pp. 164–168, who describes power in terms of resources, acts, and outcomes. The substantive content of the discussion following, however, varies substantially from Holsti's original terms, especially in the discussion of power as strategies.

[4]For a good example, see Rudolph J. Rummel, *The Dimensions of Nations* (Beverly Hills: Sage, 1972).

contrast to the focus on "objects," which underlies the concept of power as resources, the emphasis now shifts to "context" insofar as the structure of relations and the specific forms of interaction between entities are held to produce outcomes that define either *ex ante* or *ex post* the true balance or extent of power.[5] This focus on context derives from the general recognition that "capabilities," at least in the political realm, may not be fungible in exactly the same sense as, say, money is in the economic realm.[6] If this is true, then a simple rank ordering of capabilities will not identify the truly most powerful entities in a system, unless one has first assessed the structure of the situation and the resources deemed to be most valuable *in that situation*. The critical value of this approach to power as strategies, therefore, consists of making all analysis sensitive to the context within which the strategies take place and whence certain strategies may derive their efficacy.

Moving beyond both capabilities and context, the third approach to power—understood as outcomes—takes the logic one step further and focuses on *consequences* to test whether the targeted entities respond in the manner intended by the initiator. The claim of power in this approach rests simply on whether the initiator was able to influence the targeted entity to act in the desired way, even if that entails undercutting the target's own interests. Power as outcomes, therefore, seeks to derive the extent of an entity's capability not from the inputs that make it powerful or from the context within which its actions were undertaken, but rather—and more simply—from an assessment of whether the entity was able to attain its desired ends, the ends for which the exercise of power took place to begin with. The great advantage of such a concept of power is that it comports with the intuitive human sense of what it means to be powerful—getting one's way—a notion captured by Robert Dahl's now classic definition of power as the ability of *A* to get *B* to do something he

---

[5]For a sophisticated attempt at capturing the notion of power in the context of certain patterned networks of influence, see R. S. Burt, "Power in a Social Topology," in R. J. Liebert and A. W. Imershein (eds.), *Power, Paradigms, and Community Research* (Beverly Hills: Sage, 1977), pp. 251–334.

[6]On this point, and on the fungibility of power in general, see David A. Baldwin, "Power Analysis and World Politics: New Trends Versus Old Tendencies," *World Politics*, Vol. 31 (1979), pp. 161–194.

would otherwise not do.[7] Despite its attractions, however, the notion of power as outcomes also has certain limitations: these include the problems of accommodating uncertainty about *B*'s original preferences and how changes in those preferences might alter *B*'s actions irrespective of *A*'s threats or coercion.[8]

RELATING POWER TO NATIONAL POWER

These approaches to power in the abstract serve an important function in measuring *national* power in the postindustrial age: they identify the principal avenues through which to approach the problem of assessing aggregate national power. They also serve to preview the advantages and limitations that may attend various approaches to measuring national power. Based on the brief remarks above, it is possible to argue that the ideal measure of national power would be one that perfectly relates power understood as resources to power understood as outcomes in a seamless sort of way. That is, it would be wonderful to have a measure of national power that could demonstrate ineluctably that better-endowed countries always get their way in the context of encounters with lesser-endowed competitors. Such a measure would not only be intuitively satisfying, it would also have the advantage of being centered on the international distribution of capabilities—a measurable variable, at least in principle, that is upheld as significant by most international relations theorists.

The key problem, however, is that such a measure of power has been difficult to find. One study, looking at military capabilities (as a proxy for national power) on the eve of war, found that militarily stronger opponents emerged victorious less than half the time, whereas weaker opponents (measured again by strength on the eve

---

[7]Robert Dahl, "The Concept of Power," *Behavioral Science,* Vol. 2 (July 1957), p. 202, and "Power" in the *International Encyclopaedia of the Social Sciences,* Vol. XII (New York: Free Press, 1968), pp. 405–415.

[8]These and other problems are usefully reviewed in Jeffery Hart, "Three Approaches to the Measurement of Power in International Relations," *International Organization,* Vol. 30 (1976), pp. 289–305.

of war) won almost two-thirds of the conflicts they engaged in.[9] The moral of the story seems to be that greater relative power, at least when measured simply by the aggregate military power indexes that most analysts reach for when they think of the phrase "the international distribution of capabilities," seems to correlate poorly with getting one's way consistently in international wars or disputes. Organski and Kugler captured this sentiment perfectly in their discussion about great-power wars when they concluded that great powers "seem to fight, whether they are weaker, as strong as, or stronger than their opponents."[10] Relative capabilities *a priori*, at least at an aggregate level, therefore, don't seem to make a difference to outcomes like victory, or the avoidance of war, or the settlement of militarized disputes on favorable terms; in other words, they don't seem to uphold outcomes as a consistently useful measure of national power.

The failure of the better-endowed states to "win" consistently—that is, the imperfect carryover from power as resources to power as outcomes—can be explained by a variety of hypotheses: the inability of stronger states to transform their power into effective battlefield outputs; the inability of stronger states to transform their unrealized potential power in contrast to less-endowed states that may be more efficient; the lack of "will" on the part of stronger states or their relative lack of interest in the matter in dispute; and so forth.[11] These explanations focus mainly on the "paradox of unrealized power,"[12] but there is another class of explanations that attributes the failure of stronger states to get their way to the lack of fungibility of power. From this insight has often come the conclusion that generalized comparisons about national power should be eschewed in favor of cross-national comparisons carried out only within a certain "policy-

---

[9]Frank Wayman, J. David Singer, and Gary Goertz, "Capabilities, Allocations, and Success in Militarized Disputes and Wars, 1816–1976," *International Studies Quarterly*, Vol. 27 (1983), pp. 497–515.

[10]A.F.K. Organski and J. Kugler, *The War Ledger* (Chicago: University of Chicago Press, 1980), pp. 51–53.

[11]For a brief survey, see Baldwin, op. cit., pp. 163–164. See also Andrew Mack, "Why Big Nations Lose Small Wars," *World Politics*, Vol. 27, No. 2 (January 1975), pp. 175–200.

[12]Ibid.

contingency framework."[13] In other words, the conspicuously inconsistent relationship between national capabilities and political success is less a substantive issue than a methodological one. The inconsistency in this view arises primarily because resources are treated as fungible—like money—without regard to whether the resources in question are actually efficacious enough to resolve the dispute to the advantage of the presumably stronger protagonist. Given this difficulty, the advocates of the power-as-strategies school would argue the need for a shift in methodology: instead of simply attempting to relate power-as-resources to power-as-outcomes, the focus should shift to the process, relationships, and situations within which such resources and outcomes interact. Lasswell and Kaplan underscore this contention clearly when they assert that all "political analysis must be contextual, and take account of the power practices actually manifested in the concrete political situation."[14]

While the reminder that context is critical for purposes of comparing power is salutary and useful, carried to an extreme it can degenerate into "ad hocism" if the uniqueness of each situation is taken as exempting it from the application of some general yardstick for comparing national power. The best power-as-strategies proponents, therefore, would argue that the emphasis on context does not imply abandoning the search for a general measure in principle. Rather, they would urge the need to identify different and distinct yardsticks that would apply to a relatively small but specific number of issue-areas, like high politics, the economy, and the environment. In each of these issue-areas, different measures of national capacity would be regulative, thus meeting the requirements for both universal explanation—albeit on a reduced scale—and sensitivity to context and conditions.

---

[13]Harold and Margaret Sprout, *Man-Milieu Relationship Hypotheses in the Context of International Politics,* Center For International Studies, Princeton University Research Monograph (Princeton, NJ: Princeton, 1956), pp. 39–49.

[14]Harold D. Lasswell and Abraham Kaplan, *Power and Society* (New Haven: Yale University Press, 1950), p. 94.

WHAT NATIONAL CAPABILITIES MATTER MOST IN PRODUCING NATIONAL POWER?

How does one cut this Gordian knot of competing conceptions of power—understood variously as "resources," "strategies," and "outcomes"—in a way that advances the goal of developing a new template of national capability for the intelligence community? Any attempt must maintain fidelity to the purpose for which this exercise was initiated, and that consideration in turn suggests certain specific directions to be followed. The objective of developing a revised framework for assessing national power is clearly served by remaining sensitive to the need to better understand power-as-resources. This is because the intelligence community is by definition involved, at least in the first instance, in giving policymakers assessments of the national capabilities of various states, especially those likely to become potential peer competitors of the United States. Given this orientation, a concern with power understood as resources cannot be avoided, but this objective is best served *by severing all connection with any effort at relating how such power could be used to secure certain political outcomes.* The objective of the new template, in other words, must be to identify which factors matter most in producing national power, not to try to demonstrate that such power will actually enable a country to get its way in the context of some international interaction involving either another country, another subnational actor, or another transnational entity. The latter demonstration is also important, but it is best conducted as a separate "second-order" exercise that uses the relevant information derived from the power-as-resources approach but is not limited by it. In that way, the evaluation of a given country's power can be integrated with other considerations relating, for example, to the context of the engagements, the character of leadership preference and risk-taking propensities, and the relative nature of the interests involved in the dispute. Focusing on power-as-resources alone, to the neglect of the relationship between resources and outcomes, no doubt makes for an analysis of narrower scope, but it still yields great benefits for developing better methodologies for individual country (and small-*n* comparative) assessments.

Focusing on power-as-resources in the manner hitherto typical to the intelligence community, however, may not provide an adequate solution, since the focus on countries as "resource containers" helps to address some dimensions of potential power but not others. The notion of power-as-resources must, therefore, be expanded to include not only latent physical capabilities, both tangible and intangible (as the intelligence community has already begun to do), but also the all-important dimensions of external structural pressure, state performance, and ideational capability. While continuing to operate broadly *within* the general tradition of power-as-resources, the very concept of "resources" itself must thus be expanded to include what Lewis W. Snider in his insightful analysis called "power-as-performance."[15] This requires descending below the level of the "country" to the subnational level of the "state"—understood as the governing mechanism of the polity—in order to capture a view of "the state as an autonomous actor that formulates independent preferences and objectives which are not reducible to an aggregate of private preferences or the interests of a dominant class."[16] Only when the state is so captured analytically will it be possible to assess how it "attempts to implement its own objectives against resistance from politically mobilized groups in society and other actors in the global environment,"[17] and thereby serves as one of the crucial transformative variables that enables the conversion of various physical and nonmaterial resources into the effective outputs like military capability.

It might be tempting to dismiss this modification entirely on the grounds that knowledge about a country's military capabilities more than suffices to establish the extent of its national power and, as such, its standing in international politics. All the other information called for—about state capacity, state-society relations, and ideational ethos—is interesting, but is ultimately not necessary, *if adequate knowledge about a country's military capabilities can be obtained.* Such a conclusion is misleading because military capability comprises both actual and potential capability. Most assessments of military power, focusing as they do on *preexisting* military power, concentrate solely on the former variable. Such an approach is satisfactory only if it is assumed that a country's preexisting capabilities

[15]Lewis W. Snider, "Identifying The Elements of State Power," *Comparative Political Studies,* Vol. 20 (1987), p. 319.

[16]Ibid.

[17]Ibid.

are what matter in international politics. If all international conflicts were relatively short, or if all conflicts were struggles between manifestly unequal states, then a focus on preexisting military capabilities (the "immediate" balance of power) would presumably suffice to establish the international order of precedence. In these situations, all the information required would be that pertaining to a country's *extant* military power, understood to mean, of course, both "hard" factors like numbers and weapons characteristics and "soft" factors like training and leadership.

If, however, conflicts in international politics are neither short nor always between manifest unequals—as they usually are in the context of great-power rivalry—then the preexisting military capability of a country becomes only one component in the index of overall national power. In the context of long-drawn-out struggles between relatively equal powers, the ability to *mobilize national resources, "potential capability," for conversion into military instruments, "actual capability,"* becomes an equally, if not more, critical dimension of national capability.[18] Most assessments that acknowledge this fact attempt to integrate potential capabilities by scrutinizing a country's raw material stocks, the level of its technology base, its investment in R&D, and other such tangibles. This is certainly a move in the right direction, but it is as yet incomplete. What is required for completeness—at least at a logical level—is an attempt to integrate some measure of "state" capability: that is, a measure assessing the robustness and effectiveness of a country's *governing institutions* to direct the changes needed to transform its potential capability into an actual capability that would determine the outcome of a struggle with other comparably positioned countries.

It is in this context that the integration of measures relating to the external environment, state-society relations, and ideational ethos actually improves our ability to understand exactly that variable which most enthralls the realist—relative military capacity—except that in this instance, relative military capacity is discerned by evaluating not simply the stock of preexisting military assets but also the capacity to mobilize latent societal resources and transform them

---

[18]This proposition has been convincingly demonstrated in Jacek Kugler and William Domke, "Comparing the Strength of Nations," *Comparative Political Studies*, Vol. 19, No. 1 (April 1986), pp. 39–69.

into usable instruments of war. It is this perspective, deriving from a focus on militarily comparable powers, that more than any other demands that all reassessments of national power undertaken from within the power-as-resources tradition converge on the three constitutive dimensions of national capacity: national resources (which are the building blocks of national power); national performance (which refers to how state activities can enable societal resources to be converted efficiently for national ends); and military capability (which, understood finally as combat proficiency, determines the political autonomy enjoyed by a given country in the international realm).

Finally, the injunctions of the power-as-strategies school cannot be neglected, but they do recede in salience given that this analysis explicitly excludes any effort to relate a country's resources to its ability to obtain certain outcomes. Consequently, the stipulation requiring sensitivity to context will be incorporated only indirectly by recognizing that power-as-resources—no matter how widely or elaborately defined—must be assessed relative to a certain issue-area. This question speaks directly to the kind of yardstick against which the ingredients of national power are to be measured. The choice of the yardstick here is determined primarily by the theoretical judgment about what is most important when understanding national power. The best studies about the emergence of great powers in international politics suggest that national power is ultimately a product of the interaction of two components: a country's ability to dominate the cycles of economic innovation at a given point in time and, thereafter, to use the fruits of this domination to produce effective military capabilities which, in turn, reinforce existing economic advantages while producing a stable political order which, though maintained primarily for one's own strategic advantage, also provides benefits for the international system as a whole.[19]

If this represents in a nutshell the genesis and *telos* of power in international politics, then, good measures of national power ought of

[19]The most important, and illuminating, works dealing with this issue are Robert Gilpin, *War and Change in World Politics* (Cambridge: Cambridge University Press, 1981); Paul Kennedy, *The Rise and Fall of the Great Powers* (New York: Random House, 1987); and George Modelski and William R. Thompson, *Leading Sectors and World Powers* (Columbia: University of South Carolina Press, 1996).

necessity to focus on whether a country has, or is developing, the resources and the performance that could enable it to become a true great power at some future time. This implies that all candidate great powers must be judged on their efforts to invest in developing the resources that would advantage them in the competition to innovate economically. Further, one needs to assess whether their state and societal performance will allow them to make the choices they must if they are to pursue courses of action that increase the likelihood of their being able to dominate the cycles of economic innovation in order to, inter alia, generate the resources necessary to develop and field the highly sophisticated military forces effective against a variety of adversaries. In identifying these issue-areas as critical for the measurement of national power, the framework proposed in this report will focus on specifying how they might be systematically scrutinized for the purposes of creating the kind of national power profile referred to earlier.

Having situated the proposed approach to national power amidst the larger traditions of viewing power in general, the next chapter will briefly review some traditional measures of national capability before discussing how the new framework, introduced in Chapter Four and elaborated in Chapters Five through Seven, expands on the best of the traditional wisdom on the subject.

Chapter Three

REVIEWING TRADITIONAL APPROACHES TO MEASURING NATIONAL POWER

Given that power is central to international politics, it is not surprising to find most theorists of international relations advancing some means or another of measuring national capability.[1] Indeed, among all modern treatises on the subject, George Liska's *The Ways of Power* is perhaps exceptional in that it does not attempt any systematic definition of either the sources or the manifestations of national power.[2] Kenneth Waltz seems to strike a middle ground: he proposes that power "be defined in terms of the distribution of capabilities"[3] but does not specify too clearly what the components that make up each data point in the distribution ought to be, except that they should encompass "all of the following items: size of population and territory, resource endowment, economic capability, military strength, political stability and competence."[4] Hans Morgenthau is perhaps the most systematic of all modern theorists in this respect, and his approach has been followed by numerous other theorists since his work *Politics Among Nations* was first published in 1948. In

[1]This chapter is drawn substantially from four sources: Richard L. Merritt and Dina A. Zinnes, "Validity of Power Indices," *International Interactions,* Vol. 14, No. 2 (1988), pp. 141–151; Richard L. Merritt and Dina A. Zinnes, "Alternative Indexes of National Power," in Richard J. Stoll and Michael D. Ward (eds.), *Power in World Politics* (Boulder: Lynne Rienner, 1989), pp. 11–28; Charles S. Taber, "Power Capability Indexes in the Third World," in Stoll and Ward, op. cit., pp. 29–48; and Jacek Kugler and Marina Arbetman, "Choosing Among Measures of Power: A Review of the Empirical Record," in Stoll and Ward, op. cit., pp. 49–78.

[2]George Liska, *The Ways of Power* (Oxford: Basil Blackwell, 1990).

[3]Kenneth N. Waltz, *Theory of International Politics* (Reading, MA: Addison-Wesley, 1979), p. 192.

[4]Ibid., p. 131.

describing the "elements of national power," he systematically includes and assesses geography, natural resources (especially food and raw materials), industrial capacity, military preparedness (especially technology, leadership, and quantity and quality of the armed forces), population (especially the distribution and trends), national character, national morale, and the quality of diplomacy and government,[5] while warning against, among other things, efforts to attribute "to a[ny] single factor an overriding importance"[6] in the measurement of power.

This tradition of attempting to systematically assess the national power of countries continued after Morgenthau, though the difficulty of comprehensively assessing power in the manner he believed necessary has resulted in a widespread violation of his stipulation that single-factor approaches are to be avoided. In an excellent survey of various traditional approaches to measuring power, Richard L. Merritt and Dina Zinnes describe several distinctive attempts to measure power that have sought to avoid the complexity of the problem by simply focusing on a single aggregate variable. These single variables are usually intended primarily as proxies for overall national power, and their users make no effort to pretend that the variables chosen are in fact comprehensive indicators of national power. In most cases, the variables chosen have been primarily a function of convenience or because of the easy availability of data.

SINGLE-VARIABLE APPROACHES TO MEASURING NATIONAL POWER

Many analysts seeking to assess current national capabilities have focused on gross military capability as their proxy for national power: they include the political scientists Inis Claude[7] and Karl Deutsch.[8] Others like Norman Alcock and Alan Newcombe have used military

---

[5]Hans Morgenthau, *Politics Among Nations,* 4th ed. (New York: Alfred A. Knopf, 1967), pp. 106–158.

[6]Ibid., 153.

[7]Inis L. Claude, *Power and International Relations* (New York: Random House, 1962).

[8]Karl W. Deutsch, *The Analysis of International Relations* (Englewood Cliffs: Prentice-Hall, 1968).

expenditures,[9] and still others have used specific military forces: George Modelski and William Thompson, for instance, have used the size of naval forces as an indicator of projectible national power in their historical studies on the "long cycle" in international politics.[10]

In addition to military capabilities, economic indicators have also been used widely as a single-variable indicator of power, especially by those, like Klaus Knorr,[11] who have been concerned with long-term trends and shifts in capabilities. Among economic indicators, national income has been favored by the demographer Kingsley Davis[12] and by A.F.K. Organski,[13] a political scientist, as "the best index of power available,"[14] while Charles Hitch and Roland McKean have advocated the usage of a variant index, namely a country's total output or GNP.[15] After a fairly careful survey of many such alternatives, the scholar Bruce Russett[16] concluded that the total consumption of fuel and electric energy was the best single-variable measure of national power, a conclusion affirmed by Oskar Morgenstern[17] and others.

The popularity of such single-variable indicators derives mainly from their simplicity and ease of use. Those who favor them are usually not convinced about the value of multivariable indices, especially since the accompanying "theory of power" that would make such

---

[9]Norman Z. Alcock and Alan G. Newcombe, "The Perception of National Power," *Journal of Conflict Resolution,* Vol. 14 (1970), pp. 335–343.

[10]George Modelski and William R. Thompson, *Seapower in Global Politics, 1494–1983* (Seattle: University of Washington Press, 1987).

[11]Klaus Knorr, *The War Potential of Nations* (Princeton: Princeton University Press, 1956).

[12]Kinsgley Davis, "The Demographic Foundations of National Power," in Morrow Berger et al. (eds.), *Freedom and Control in Modern Society* (New York: Farrar, Straus & Giroux, 1954), pp. 206–242.

[13]A.F.K. Organski, *World Politics* (New York: Knopf, 1958).

[14]Ibid., p. 436.

[15]Charles Hitch and Roland McKean, *The Economics of Defense in the Nuclear Age* (Cambridge: Harvard University Press, 1960).

[16]Bruce M. Russett, "Is There a Long-Run Trend Towards Concentration in the International System?" *Comparative Political Studies,* Vol. 1 (1968), pp. 103–122.

[17]Oskar Morgenstern et al., *Long Term Projections of Political and Military Power* (Cambridge: Ballinger, 1973).

measures meaningful is often either not advanced or, even when advanced, fails to command widespread acceptance. Given this perception, most advocates of single-variable indices appear to be satisfied that their measures are sufficient for the purposes to which they are directed, mainly a rank ordering of countries according to national capacity. Despite their widespread popularity, single-variable indicators are nonetheless often criticized, especially by mathematically sophisticated scholars, for their lack of realism. Not surprisingly, therefore, several multivariable approaches to measuring national power have also been advanced over the years.

MULTIVARIABLE APPROACHES TO MEASURING NATIONAL POWER

The earliest and perhaps most influential multivariable measure was advanced in 1956 by Klaus Knorr in his classic work, *The War Potential of Nations*. Seeking to ascertain the ability of a country "to provide quantities of military manpower and supplies in the event of war,"[18] Knorr was drawn to a wide variety of factors that could be summarized by the categories of economic capacity, administrative competence, and motivation for war. Despite identifying numerous critical ingredients under each of these categories, Knorr did not provide any "model" to suggest how these factors might be combined. His work was nonetheless seminal in that it provided the foundations on which several theorists would later develop alternate solutions.

A complex nonlinear multivariable index that attempted to both identify discrete variables and specify their interrelationships came in 1960 with the work of Clifford German, who produced a world power index that took the following form:

$$G = \text{national power} = N(L + P + I + M),$$

where N is nuclear capability, L is land, P is population, I is the industrial base, and M is military size.[19] Each of these variables was

[18]Knorr, op. cit., p. 41.

[19]F. Clifford German, "A Tentative Evaluation of World Power," *Journal of Conflict Resolution*, Vol. 4 (1960) pp. 138–144.

further broken down into a series of factors, each of which was scored by a variety of criteria pertinent to the factor concerned. After reviewing this model, Merritt and Zinnes concluded that "of all the power indexes considered, the German index is the most complex. It consists of a multitude of variables, both summational and syntality, a series of scoring schemes, and several instances in which judgments must be made."[20] A similar nonlinear (but somewhat simpler) multivariable index was subsequently proposed by Wilhelm Fucks in 1965, who sought to derive national power from three summational variables—population size (p), energy production (z), and steel production (z_1)—arranged in one of nine formulas for measuring national power (M), all of which were variants of one another and took the form of $M = p^2z$, $M = p^{3/2}z$, etc.[21]

In contrast to the nonlinear measures of German and Fucks, Norman Alcock and Alan Newcombe in 1970 advanced a straightforward linear index of popular perceptions of national power that also utilized multiple variables. Using regression analyses on three variables, per-capita GNP, population, and population density, they attempted to rank the relative power of scores of countries in the context of popular perceptions of national strength. A similar linear index of capabilities, but one focusing on real national assets as opposed to the perception of those assets, was devised by J. David Singer's Correlates of War project and published in 1972.[22] Here too, population (understood both in terms of total and levels of urban population), industrial capacity (understood in terms of energy consumption and iron and steel production), and military capabilities (understood in terms of military expenditures and force size) were added up to provide values for a particular country, which were then assessed as a percentage of the global total. Another effort along similar lines was pursued by Wayne Ferris, who constructed an index in 1973 that sought to "provide scores on the capabilities of nearly all states in the

---

[20]Merritt and Zinnes (1989), op. cit., p. 22.

[21]Wilhelm Fucks, *Formeln zur Macht: Prognosen uber Volker, Wirtschaft Potentiale* (Verlags-Anstalt, 1965).

[22]J. David Singer et al., "Capability Distribution, Uncertainty, and Major-Power War," in Bruce Russett (ed.), *Peace, War and Numbers* (Beverly Hills: Sage, 1972), pp. 19–48. See also Stuart A. Bremer, "National Capabilities and War Pronenes," in J. David Singer (ed.), *The Correlates of War II: Testing Some* Realpolitik *Models* (New York: Free Press, 1980).

system relative to nearly all other states"[23] during the period 1850–1966. This effort focused on six variables—land area, total population, government revenue, defense expenditures, value of international trade, and the size of the armed forces—in an effort to produce a historical comparison of international power for literally scores of countries.

Finally, among the more widely recognized indexes of national power was the one devised by Ray Cline in 1975. This nonlinear, multivariable index attempted to integrate both capabilities and commitment to create a formula that would rank order the perceived power of states. Cline's formula was

$$P_p = (C + E + M)\ (S + W),$$

where C is critical mass (including population and territory), E is economic capacity (including income plus energy plus nonfuel minerals plus manufacturing plus food plus trade), M is military capacity (including the strategic balance plus combat capabilities plus a bonus for effort), S is the national strategy coefficient, and W is national will (including the level of national integration, the strength of leadership, and the relevance of strategy to the national interest). The formula won a wide readership both in academia and within the defense community, and some variants of it were used to develop the U.S. Army's estimates of long-range trends in the international system.

A SUMMARY OF TRADITIONAL APPROACHES TO MEASURING NATIONAL POWER

Clearly, this brief survey suggests that there have been numerous efforts to measure the aggregate power of states throughout the postwar period. These efforts no doubt seem to have been concentrated during the 1960s and the 1970s, when the social sciences in general and political science in particular appeared to be maturing as disciplines in the United States. Since the late 1970s, no new attempts at developing aggregate power measures of the kinds illus-

---

[23]W. Ferris, *The Power Capabilities of Nation-States* (Lexington: Lexington, 1973), p. 58.

trated above have materialized (or at least none have received widespread visibility), in part because such aggregate measures have been perceived as having reached the limits of their success. Scholarship since then seems to have focused on either using the preexisting measures of power to answer other questions—like, for example, those relating to the onset of war, the problems of escalation, and the relationships between capability and the outcomes of conflicts—or to refine the preexisting measures through better quantitative techniques. Only recently has a younger group of scholars like Jacek Kugler, William Domke, and Lewis Snider begun to revisit the vexing question of power, but their pathbreaking work has focused not on creating aggregate indices of national power per se—as the scholars of the 1960s and 1970s had done—but rather on deepening the notion of national power to include measures of capacity relating to the societal realm. Before their work is reviewed and integrated, however, it is worth summarizing what the scholarship of the earlier generation set out to do in its measures of national power and what it achieved.

The traditional approaches to measuring national power may be summarized in the following way.

First, most traditional approaches of the sort identified above sought to *rank order* the status of countries in terms of their capacity for war. The objective in most cases, thus, consisted of charting the international warrant of precedence, or the hierarchy of capabilities in the international system, based on the premise that the capacity for war was what ultimately distinguished the power of one country from another. At least one approach—Singer's *Correlates of War*—sought to correlate national capability with certain kinds of political outcomes, but this work is the exception to the above rule.

Second, while the various indexes can be distinguished in terms of the number of variables employed and how these relate internally, the most conspicuous characteristic of the traditional approaches is their diversity. That is, each index differs from the others in terms of the number of states assessed, the time frames of comparison, and the complexity of formulae employed.

Third, most indexes incorporate only summational elements, that is, material elements that can be simply added, in various combinations. In large part, this is because "syntality" variables that measure qualitative issues like the characteristics of groups or elites are difficult to capture in a uniform and systematic way, though Cline's world power formula certainly stands out as an exception.

Fourth, most of the indexes focus mainly on the "country" as the appropriate unit of analysis. The country here is treated as a "resource container"[24] possessing certain measurable contents which, if appropriately identified and measured, yield an understanding of its inherent capability. With the exception again of Cline's index, which seeks to capture dimensions of national integration and leadership strength, no traditional approach descended "below" the subnational level to examine either political institutions or ideational ethos.

Fifth, most of the indices used in the traditional indexes of power are invariably gross indices. Even measures of military capability largely consist of gross measures like the size of inventory or the numbers of specific pieces of equipment. Both the assets counted and the resources identified as salient are clearly those that acquired significance in the industrial age, when variables like the level of steel production, the extent of energy consumed, and the size of food stocks mattered much more than they had before.

Assessing these approaches synoptically with a view to discerning whether there are any significant differences in their results, Merritt and Zinnes reach some interesting conclusions.[25] To begin with, they find that most studies yield similar findings in terms of their rank ordering of national capabilities. Thus, irrespective of the variables measured or the formula of measurement employed, the most powerful countries in the system turn out to be the same across all indexes. Further, when some of the approaches attempt to measure the absolute amounts of power possessed by countries, the findings across studies seem to be even more congruent than the findings

---

[24]For an analysis of the limitations of the traditional realist view of countries as "resource containers," see Ashley J. Tellis, *The Drive to Domination: Towards a Pure Realist Theory of Politics*, Vol. II, unpublished Ph.D. dissertation, p. 259ff. For a survey of how territoriality has been understood by several modern schools in political science, see also Gary Goertz and Paul F. Diehl, *Territorial Changes and International Conflict* (London: Routledge, 1992), pp. 1–32.

[25]Merritt and Zinnes (1989), op. cit., pp. 23–26.

based on rank-ordered scores. In all cases, however, the similarity of findings is greatest for the developed world and least for the developing world—an outcome generally attributed to analysts' greater interest in and familiarity with the great powers as opposed to the underdeveloped countries. Charles Taber suggests, however, that this lack of a "good fit" for developing countries may arise because of structural reasons, like an oversimplification of some attributes, the noncomparability of some indicators for theoretical or empirical reasons, the greater fluctuations in the developing world with respect to some attributes, and perhaps even the unreliability of data in some instances.[26] Finally, and most fascinatingly, no essential difference is discerned in the findings between single-variable and multivariable indexes. This leads to the stark, but devastating, conclusion reached by Merritt and Zinnes that, in several of the indexes reviewed, "needless additional data and arithmetic computation have been introduced without an[y] increase in payoff."[27]

This conclusion delivers a cautionary reminder to all future efforts at reconceptualizing national power. The following chapter will briefly assess the limitations and the value of these traditional approaches as a prelude to elaborating a revised view of how national power ought to be conceived for the specific purpose of creating the standardized power profile through which a small number of candidate great powers may be synchronically and diachronically compared.

---

[26]Taber, op. cit., pp. 42–44.

[27]Merritt and Zinnes (1989), op. cit., p. 26.

Chapter Four

TOWARD A REVISED VIEW OF MEASURING NATIONAL POWER

The finding that single-variable measures of power turn out to be just as effective as more complex indexes for purposes of rank ordering countries—even when they focus on entirely different variables altogether—suggests that exercises in rank ordering may not indicate very much about what makes countries "really" powerful. Such exercises point to how countries compare against one another by some gross measures, but they are not grounded in a clear understanding of what makes certain nations powerful or why some nations can be said to have more power than others. Further, in focusing on rank ordering to the neglect of almost all else, the traditional approaches to measuring power offered an "extensive" rather than "intensive" picture that depicts the global distribution of capabilities but does not enable a close and detailed scrutiny of any specific target country. Finally, most traditional indexes fail to incorporate qualitative factors that describe state capacity, presumably the most important variable that recent research suggests must be incorporated in any adequate assessment of individual national capabilities.

The key limitation of the traditional approaches, therefore, is not that they are wrong but that their methodology is inappropriate for *intensively* investigating the national power of a few candidate great powers of specific interest to the United States.

ASSESSING THE POWER CAPABILITY OF SPECIFIC TARGET COUNTRIES

For the intelligence community, developing a universal hierarchy of national power capabilities is an interesting effort, but one that is clearly of secondary importance. The primary objective must be to assess the power capability of a few critical countries, one at a time. These countries must be investigated "intensively" in order to assess both the extent and the depth of their capabilities, and such investigations must proceed in accordance with some standardized "template" so as to enable both diachronic comparisons of progress and synoptic comparisons among a small group of peers. The conceptual underpinnings of this template are inspired by the work of Schumpeter,[1] Rostow,[2] Gilpin,[3] Kennedy,[4] and Modelski and Thompson[5] and are depicted in Figure 1.

This graphic suggests that national power is ultimately a product of the interaction of two components: a country's ability to dominate the cycles of economic innovation at a given point in time and, thereafter, to utilize the fruits of this domination to produce effective military capabilities. Those capabilities in turn reinforce existing economic advantages while producing a stable political order which, though maintained primarily for the country's own strategic advantage, also provides benefits for the international system as a whole. The ability to dominate the cycles of innovation in the international economy is the critical mainspring beneath the production of power: this implies that national power has fundamentally *material* components, without which all other manifestations would be devoid of substance. More importantly, however, the ability to innovate—understood in the Schumpeterian sense as the creation of new products and methods of production, the opening of new markets and the

---

[1]Joseph A. Schumpeter, *Theory of Economic Development* (Cambridge: Harvard University Press, 1934), and Joseph A. Schumpeter, *Business Cycles* (New York: McGraw Hill, 1939).

[2]Walt W. Rostow, *The Stages of Economic Growth,* and Walt W. Rostow, *The World Economy* (Austin: University of Texas Press, 1980).

[3]Gilpin, op. cit.

[4]Kennedy, op. cit.

[5]Modelski and Thompson, op. cit. (1996).

Figure 1—Explaining the Generation of National Power

discovery of new raw materials, and the pioneering of new forms of commercial organization[6]—is critical precisely because it allows for *differential rates of capital accumulation between states.*

Thanks to the interrelatedness of all economic activity, major innovations typically appear "clustered" at particular times and in particular economic sectors. This clustering arises because important innovations usually spawn multiple, derivative improvements which grow out of the "creative disequilibrium" that emerges whenever any significantly new products, processes, and organizations forms are introduced in society. Over time, these clusters of related innovations give rise to a new "leading sector" of economic activity that sustains itself mainly because the new innovations, generating supernormal profits, tend to discourage investment in other sectors of the economy in the initial phases of the product cycle. The new leading sector—fueled principally by the outgrowth of productive activities generated by the new innovation—then tends to slowly supplant previously dominant industries and drives a powerful expansion of the economy which, over time, produces consequential effects that reverberate throughout the international economic system. While these effects usually take the form of technology diffusion, product and process imitation, and derivative innovation, the strategic consequences of the generative innovations are that they enable—at least temporarily—productive superiority in the originating country. This superiority derives from the fact that the new leading sectors are, at least initially, concentrated in the countries in which the original innovations occurred, and "it is precisely th[is] uneven dis-

---

[6]Schumpeter, op. cit. (1934), p. 66.

tribution of innovation at the core that causes temporary gaps between different countries."[7]

How certain countries come to achieve dominance in some leading sectors is a complex phenomenon that cannot be examined here in any detail. Suffice it to say that the evidence suggests that entities achieving such dominance in the past were those with:

- relatively efficient domestic markets that enabled smooth access to resources and credit;
- relatively open societies that encouraged economic innovation and encouraged creativity;
- relatively ordered institutional arrangements for safeguarding property rights and ensuring peaceful dispute resolution;
- conscientious political leadership that valued power and control in international politics;
- sensitivity to global competition and responsiveness to the international problems of the time.[8]

The evidence also suggests that dominance of the leading sector is never permanent or timeless, as diffusion, imitation, and competitive innovations occurring elsewhere combine with the ubiquitous phenomenon of diminishing returns to account for both the decline of preexisting economic leaders and the rise of new commercial competitors.[9] This phenomenon implies that the nature of the leading sectors will change over time and that all measures of national power must, therefore, allow the performance of potential competitors to be measured relative to both the leading sectors at present—in order

---

[7]Nicole Bousquet, "From Hegemony to Competition: Cycles of the Core?" in Terence K. Hopkins and Immanuel Wallerstein (eds.), *Processes of the World-System* (Beverly Hills: Sage, 1980), p. 52.

[8]Modelski and Thompson, op. cit. (1996), pp. 51–62. See also William R. Thompson, "Uneven Economic Growth, Systemic Challenges, and Global Wars," *International Studies Quarterly*, Vol. 27 (1983), pp. 341–355.

[9]For one reading of the mechanics underlying this process, see Bousquet, op. cit. For others, see Karen A. Rasler and William R. Thompson, "War and the Economic Growth of Major Powers," *American Journal of Political Science*, Vol. 29 (1985), pp. 513–538, and Christopher Chase-Dunn and Joan Sokolovsky, "Interstate System and Capitalist World-Economy," *International Studies Quarterly*, Vol. 27, No. 3 (1983), pp. 19–42.

to assess the effects of diffusion and imitation, if any—and the leading sectors of the future—a difficult exercise that involves, among other things, continual sensitivity to the kinds of innovations that appear poised to form the leading sectors of tomorrow.[10]

Irrespective of how successful these analytic efforts may be, the fact remains that the uneven distribution of innovations generally accounts for why some countries are able to secure superior rates of capital accumulation, and the historical record illustrated in Figure 2 seems to suggest that—as a slight twist on Mackinder might have it—"who dominates the leading sectors, dominates the world."

THE RELATIONSHIP AMONG ECONOMIC INNOVATION, MILITARY CAPABILITIES, AND HEGEMONY

Even though the advantages in capital accumulation accruing as a result of successful innovations may never be permanent over historical time, they are usually substantial enough to allow their possessors to utilize these resources to develop "hegemonic potential" in the form of effective military forces. As Bousquet noted succinctly,

> thanks to these major innovations, the entity wherein they occur finds itself in a position of production supremacy within the world-economy, and eventually obtains other dimensions characteristic of authentic hegemony, namely commercial and financial supremacy, and political leadership coupled with military supremacy.[11]

In a power-political sense, therefore, the ultimate value in being able to dominate the leading sectors of the global economy is that it makes attaining and maintaining hegemony possible. It has already been demonstrated, for example, that securing an early lead in the cycle of innovation is critical for producing hegemony because initial economic dominance usually allows the innovating state to fend off later challengers.[12] These challengers no doubt arise for all the rea-

---

[10]A good example of such an effort can be found in Steven W. Popper, Caroline S. Wagner, and Eric V. Larson, *New Forces at Work* (Santa Monica, CA: RAND, MR-1008-OSTP, 1998).

[11]Bousquet, op. cit. (1980), p. 79.

[12]Modelski and Thompson, op. cit. (1996), pp. 65–118.

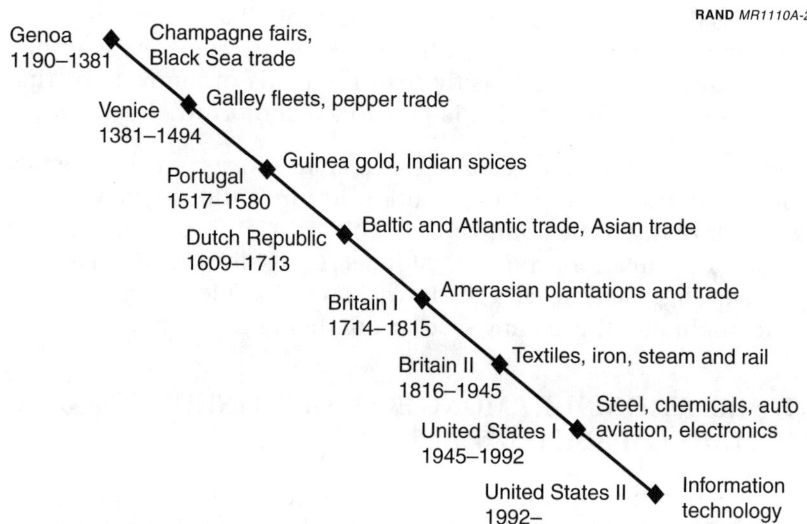

SOURCE: George Modelski and William R. Thompson, *Leading Sectors and World Powers* (Columbia: University of South Carolina Press, 1996), p. 69.

Figure 2—"Leading Sectors" Underlying Hegemonic Control in History

sons alluded to earlier, but their inability to match the early innovator's advantages in accumulated economic resources results—or, at least, has resulted historically—in a failure to successfully replace any extant hegemonies through war.[13] This outcome may also obtain because "the country creating a major cluster of innovations often finds immediate military applications and [both] propels itself to hegemonic status [and maintains that status] by that mechanism as well."[14]

The causal logic underlying the production of hegemony illustrated in Figure 1 allows for the possibility that innovations in military power could—through the mechanisms of war and conquest—allow a country to achieve hegemony even before, properly speaking, it dominates the cycles of innovation in the international economy. In

[13]Thompson, op. cit. (1983), pp. 348–351.

[14]Joshua S. Goldstein, *Long Cycles: Prosperity and War in the Modern Age* (New Haven: Yale University Press, 1988), p. 140.

fact, as early as 1941, barely a few years after Schumpeter's path-breaking work on economic innovation was published, Albert Rose argued that "modern war may [in fact] be the innovation par excellence in the Schumpeterian system, and as such, the dominant cause of long waves in economic activity."[15] There is no reason in principle why military innovation—rather than economic innovation—cannot allow a candidate great power to secure control of the international system as a prelude to reorganizing that system in order to sustain future economic dominance as a precondition for continued hegemonic control.[16] Consequently, the emphasis on mastery over economic processes in this analysis (rather than over military capabilities *ab initio*) ought to be viewed primarily as a methodological point of entry into the overall logic, which is cyclic and mutually reinforcing and can be explicated in either direction: enduring great power capabilities, and by implication claims to political hegemony, can be *generated* either as a result of domination over the cycles of innovation in the international economy or as a result of the creation of hegemonic potential in the form of superior military capabilities. Ensuring that the hegemony generated as a result of either of these processes *endures*, however, requires the country in question—sooner or later—to *both* dominate the cycles of economic innovation and sustain the production of superior military capabilities. In the final instance, the latter simply cannot be assured without achieving the former.

Having admitted this, however, the production of effective military instruments, usually as a result of (or in tandem with) the predominance established in the economic realm, remains important for hegemony because military forces remain the final arbiter of disputes in the "anarchic" realm of international politics. The country that has the most effective military instruments—understood as an amalgam of technology, doctrine, training, and organization—can shape the operations of the international system to its advantage: it can define and enforce, as it were, "the rules of the game." This is in

---

[15]Albert Rose, "Wars, Innovations and Long Cycles," *American Economic Review*, Vol. 31 (1941), p. 105.

[16]As Thompson, op. cit. (1983, p. 347) notes, for example, in the context of early modern Europe, "it has not always been a truism, contrary to [Paul] Kennedy, that naval strength depends upon economic strength for naval strength was required first to facilitate the very creation of much of the global elite's newfound wealth."

fact the most useful conceptualization of the meaning of hegemony in international politics, since it shifts the emphasis away from simple balances of capability to what such balances produce in terms of power-political effects.[17] Since international politics remains a realm without a formal authority, order is produced ultimately by those entities capable of dominating the system by force, that is, countries that can develop and field highly sophisticated military forces capable of performing the most demanding military operations that might have to be mounted against a diverse variety of adversaries. Countries that have military forces of such puissance can use these coercive capabilities to both reinforce the existing economic and political concentrations of power in the system and sustain alliance arrangements and international regimes that favor their interests. This implies that the military capabilities of most interest to a framework that seeks to measure national power are those which are readily usable in the customary violence of international politics and which promise effective dominance over a country's most significant competitors.

These brief remarks about the substantive underpinnings of the framework advanced in this report are intended to emphasize the following issues.

First, it is assumed that countries will remain the most important units of the international system in comparison to individuals, non-government actors, and transnational organizations, at least where issues of "high politics"—those issues relating to order and governance—are concerned. In this environment, countries will continue as the ultimate arbiters of their own political choices, and while these choices will be limited by the actions and capabilities of others, countries will nonetheless continue to employ power in defense of their own interests.

Second, while the roots of national power no doubt derive from a country's ability to dominate the leading sectors of the global economy, the most important manifestation of power will continue to be military capability because it pertains to the domain of survival and conditions the freedom of action enjoyed by entities in an environ-

---

[17]Goldstein, op. cit., p. 281ff.

ment where there is no other overarching ideological or moral constraint on national action.

Third, where military capability is concerned, the ability to conduct diverse conventional operations effectively will remain critical because, even though nuclear weapons have become the *ultima ratio regum* in international politics, their relative inefficacy in most situations other than those involving national survival implies that their utility will continue to be significant but highly restricted. The ability to conduct different and sophisticated forms of conventional warfare will, therefore, remain the critical index of national power because of its undiminished utility, flexibility, responsiveness, and credibility.[18]

Thanks to changes in technology and in the mode of production more generally, the ability to conduct *efficacious* conventional warfare, however, will increasingly depend on a country's ability to incorporate emerging technologies in its military operations, especially its ability to master "information-dominant" operations. While the full extent of what is entailed by this locution is as yet unclear, it is becoming more and more obvious that the ability to exploit the information technology revolution will bequeath its possessors great advantages, especially relative to competitors who may still be locked in the pursuit of the attrition and maneuver strategies followed in the past.[19] The ability to engage in such operations effectively, thus, not only promises to increase the power capabilities of a country relative to competitors who engage in an older mode of warfighting, but it also promises to advantage a country against competitors who may either use "information-dominant" operations less effectively or lack the structural depth to engage in such competition intensively over a long period. Arguably, "information-dominant" operations in the context of conventional warfare may also offer some advantages even against competitors armed with small numbers of nuclear weapons or other weapons of mass destruction, and they arguably

[18]William J. Perry, "Desert Storm and Deterrence," *Foreign Affairs,* Vol. 70, No. 4 (1991), pp. 66–82.

[19]John Arquilla, "The Strategic Implications of Information Dominance," *Strategic Review* (Summer 1994), pp. 24–30.

offer other kinds of advantages in "low-intensity conflicts" and in "operations other than war" as well.[20]

The ability to conduct "information-dominant" operations in the context of conventional warfare implies that, when measuring national power, attention ought to focus ultimately on assessing a country's *warfighting capabilities*, understood at least in terms of combat proficiency. This proficiency, in turn, ought to be metered by a force's ability to effectively conduct the most complex military operations possible given the technologies, doctrines, and organizational forms available to it today or potentially available in the foreseeable future. Because the most potent and flexible conventional warfighting capabilities are the ones that require information-exploiting technologies in various forms—from advanced sensor systems at one end, through flexible and redundant command and control systems, all the way to sophisticated weapons and munitions—the methodology for assessing combat proficiency used by the framework offered in this report implicitly reflects an interest in assessing whether a country is integrating, would be interested in integrating, or is capable of integrating advanced information-intensive technologies into its armed forces.

On balance, therefore, the template for assessing national power offered in this report is based on the presumption that because the "leading sector" today—information and communications technology—affects the economic, political, and strategic capabilities of a country in very significant ways, a comprehensive scrutiny of national power must begin by assessing whether a country can participate in the evolving knowledge revolution, and to what degree, and end by assessing whether it is pursuing efforts to translate (or is capable of translating) the fruits of this revolution into effective military capabilities.

DEFINING NATIONAL POWER

National power can be defined simply as a country's capacity to pursue strategic goals through purposeful action. This view of national

[20]Jeffery R. Cooper, *Applying Information Technologies to Low-Intensity Conflicts: A "Real-Time Information Shield" Concept* (Arlington: SRS Technologies, 1992).

power suggests two distinct but related dimensions of capacity: an external dimension, which consists of a nation's capacity to affect the global environment through its economic, political, and military potential, and an internal dimension, which consists of a nation's capacity to transform the resources of its society into "actionable knowledge" that produces the best civilian and military technologies possible. Any effort at creating a useful national power profile must incorporate variables that capture these two dimensions.

The revised framework for measuring national power, illustrated in Figure 3, attempts to capture both these dimensions of national power in terms of three distinct realms.

The first realm, "national resources," seeks to capture the "building blocks" a country needs if it is to develop modes of production that enable it to dominate the cycles of innovation in the global economy and increase its hegemonic potential through the creation of highly sophisticated military forces capable of effectively executing the most demanding military operations against a diverse variety of adversaries. Since the beginning of the current international system, these "building blocks" have usually been measured by variables such as population, size of territory, economic strength (usually

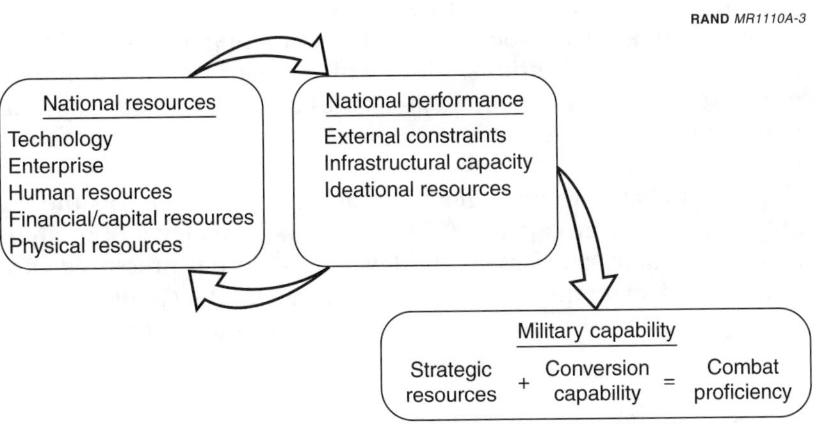

Figure 3—A Revised View of National Power

measured in terms of GNP/GDP), and natural resources.[21] Not surprisingly, these are the indicators commonly identified by the traditional approaches to measuring power, and they cannot be—and have not been—simply jettisoned. They remain important and, more critically, indicate the thresholds through which countries must pass if they are to become important political and military actors in the international system. Consequently, they are incorporated in this revised framework for measuring national power, but in the context of other, newer qualitative variables that speak to a country's wider ability to incorporate a science-based knowledge revolution in its economic life. This ability to incorporate newer and ever more effective forms of "actionable knowledge" in every realm of material life is critical because it contributes to creating the foundations for new forms of military power. The "building blocks" of national power identified in this framework are therefore discussed here under the rubric of (1) technology, (2) enterprise, (3) human resources, (4) financial/capital resources, and (5) physical resources.

The second realm, "national performance," seeks to capture the mechanisms that enable countries to convert the "building blocks" identified in the first realm, which represent latent power, into tangible forms of usable power. The objective of introducing this dimension of national power is to move beyond the traditional view of countries as "bordered power-containers"[22] to something that models them as active social structures consisting of state and societal actors and institutions, all of which exist in an environment populated by many similar such entities abroad. Introducing this dimension allows the framework to capture an element that most traditional measures of power do not accommodate: the relationship a state has with its own society and the consequences thereof for national power capability. In particular, this level of analysis allows the analyst to assess the levels of external pressures confronting a given country as well as how aware and responsive a particular state-society complex is to the new resources that must be

---

[21]Jack S. Levy, *War in the Modern Great Power System, 1495–1975,* Lexington, KY: University Press of Kentucky, 1983; A.F.K. Organski, *World Politics;* Waltz, *Theory of International Politics.*

[22]Anthony Giddens, *The Nation-State and Violence* (Berkeley: University of California Press, 1985), p. 121.

produced if it is to develop the capability to both dominate the cycles of innovation and transform that dominance into effective hegemonic potential. Including variables like the infrastructural and ideational capacity of a country enables the analyst to characterize the state's capacity for: *discerning* the most appropriate socio-technical production choices for augmenting its own power in the face of the prevailing and prospective challenges imposed by both economic processes and international competition; *developing* the appropriate resources to dominate both the cycles of innovation and the processes of international politics; and, finally, *transforming* existing resources into effective capital instruments for securing favorable outcomes in both the productive and the coercive arenas internationally. At this level of "national performance," the three variables to be examined are: (1) the external constraints emerging from the international system, (2) the infrastructural capacity of a given state, and (3) its ideational resources.

The third realm, "military capability," seeks to capture the manifest signs of national power that are ultimately personified by the combat proficiency of a country's military force. Military capabilities may be treated almost as the "outputs" of national power production process because they represent the effective coercive strength that a country can bring to bear against any competitors, which is, in the "anarchic" system of international politics, its first line of defense. In the framework illustrated in Figure 3, military capabilities are understood to be a resultant product of the continual, cyclic, *interaction* of both national resources and national performance: resources may be "building blocks," but these building blocks, far from existing in nature, must be consciously produced as a result of human artifice, which is captured, however imperfectly, by the domain of national performance. The institutions inhabiting this latter realm, in turn, rely on the resources they have produced both to maintain themselves internally and to expand their own (or their country's) power externally, and the most important manifestation of this external power is military capability. Many traditional indexes of national power incorporated military capabilities in some form or another, though this was usually done through the use of summary variables like the levels of military expenditure or the gross size of the armed forces. The kind of capabilities focused on in this framework seek a greater level of detail. Toward that end, the examination of military capability as a vector of national power is patterned analogously to the larger framework for assessing national power. It identifies:

- The strategic resources a military receives from the government it serves, which include defense budgets, manpower, military infrastructure, combat RDT&E institutions, the defense industrial base, and the warfighting inventory and support;
- The variables bearing upon the means by which these resources are converted into effective capabilities—for example, the threats facing a country and the strategy developed to cope with them, the structure of civil-military relations, the density of foreign military-to-military relations, the nature of doctrine, training, and organization, and the potential and capacity for innovation; and
- The capabilities of the combat force itself, understood via a spectrum of warfighting competencies which may be attained to a greater or lesser degree and which may be compared across countries.

In viewing national power in this disaggregated way, it is important to recognize the three distinctive features of this approach. First, while the "country" remains the nominal unit of analysis, it is in fact *decomposed* into many constituent parts like state and society, each of which has relative capabilities to be gauged. Thus, for example, the quality of the societal base is assessed in the realm of national resources when the level of technology present, the innovativeness of its entrepreneurs, and the skills and quality of its population as represented by its human capital are assessed. Societal character also surfaces in the context of national performance when a nation's ideational resources in the form of its commitment to wealth and power are assessed. Similarly, state capacity, understood as the effectiveness of a country's governing institutions, is also scrutinized directly in the realm of national performance where, under the rubric of infrastructural capacity, the examination focuses on how legitimate the state is, the extent to which it penetrates society, and how well it can extract resources from society for its own ends. This argument, that the social structures of a country matter in any assessment of national power, implies *a fortiori* that the state-society complex is itself an element in the production of a country's power and therefore that national power capabilities cannot be treated as exogenous to the ordering structures within a country. The systematic inclusion of such a variable should make the suggested measures more sensitive to the changing nature of power in the postindustrial age. Besides such novel elements, the framework also incorporates more traditional measures, such as those relating to geography when it includes raw physical resources as one component of overall national power.

Second, while the country as the nominal unit of analysis is decomposed in the manner described above to provide a more fine-grained assessment of national power, the *interdependencies* within its various internal components are also implicitly recognized. Thus, for example, while the societal base may be examined in terms of the levels of technology present, the extent of innovativeness among its entrepreneurs, and the skills and quality of its population as represented by its human capital, there is no doubt that these societal attributes are also clearly a product in some sense or another of specific *state* choices and actions. By expanding the notion of resources beyond physical assets to include such broad attributes, the framework implicitly argues that the most useful resources in the postindustrial age may not necessarily be natural resources and, consequently, that any useful assessment of national power in the postindustrial age must account for the underpinnings of such power from the oft-forgotten perspective of the capital production choices that any given state makes. By treating resources in the broadest sense possible, this framework then explicitly incorporates interdependency between state and society and thus can help account for how aware and responsive a state-society complex must be to the new resources it will have to *produce*, if the country is to simultaneously sustain a productive society at the leading edge of economic innovation and keep up with the changing demands of adequacy as military technology, doctrine, organization, and concepts of operation continue to rapidly evolve.

Third, while the broad relationship between state and society is incorporated within this organizing framework, the framework itself is indifferent to any particular normative model of state-society relations. Following Katzenstein's pathbreaking work on the subject,[23] it has become customary among many scholars of international politics, especially political realists, to define national strength by reference to the degree of political and economic centralization, such that the existence of centralized political systems is automatically treated as making for stronger countries. This view of national power, deriving in large part from the experience of the rise of absolute monarchies in early modern Europe, however, produces explanatory anomalies. The most conspicuous anomaly remains the United States, a powerful country which by Katzenstein's criteria possesses both a weak state and a weak society. The United States, however, is just one of many such anomalies because, as Kugler's and Domke's research has demonstrated, there appears to be no systematic relationship between political centralization and a country's national power, especially when understood ultimately as its military capacity.[24] This finding should not be entirely surprising, because both the United States and Great Britain before it remain powerful examples of weak states that nonetheless produced immense national power, both in economic terms and as manifested through a powerful military. The relevant criterion for national power may therefore not be whether a country has a strong or a weak state in relation to its society, but whether it has a *minimally effective state*—irrespective of what state capacities relative to its society may be. This framework, therefore, seeks to explore the predicates of a minimally effective state without in any way privileging strong states–weak societies or strong societies–weak states (or any other combination, for that matter) as normatively desirable for the production of national power.

While such a framework is intended to be comprehensive precisely because it is meant—eventually—to function as the conceptual foundation for a "national power profile" that can be used to "measure" and "compare" the capabilities of a few candidate great powers of interest to the United States, the template as depicted in Figure 3 does not incorporate any system of internal weights that prioritizes one set of variables relative to another. While it would be

---

[23]Peter J. Katzenstein, "Conclusion: Domestic Structures and Strategies of Economic Policy," *International Organization,* Vol. 31, No. 4 (Autumn 1977), pp. 879–920.

[24]Kugler and Domke, op. cit., p. 40.

useful, other things being equal, to have such a weighting system, developing one that is both universal and coherent is extremely difficult and perhaps impossible. It may also be unnecessary so long as the objective is to develop *evaluative* measures of national power. The meaning of "evaluative" in this context is the opposite of "automatic": since the framework is not intended to replicate a mechanical computer but rather to provide an ordering structure that helps regional or national analysts to systematically reach and compare judgments about the power capabilities of a few states, it is hoped that the users themselves would supply—either explicitly or implicitly—any weights they believe are justified on the basis of their knowledge of a specific country. This framework aims to simply identify those variables that arguably are critically necessary for the production of national power in the postindustrial age: collecting empirical data relating to the variables identified in the framework would assist in the formation of more sophisticated judgments about national capability and would allow observers to go beyond simple indicators like GNP or military capital stocks when faced with assertions that some "candidate great powers" may or may not be poised to materialize as true peer competitors of the United States.[25]

With this as a backdrop, the next three chapters elaborate the revised framework for measuring national power in three distinct realms: national resources, national performance, and military capability.

---

[25]The appendix in this report seeks to assist this process by providing a short list of the most important indicators of national power in the postindustrial age. These indicators are based on the template offered in Figure 3, and to the degree that they represent the minimally necessary information requirements for judging national capabilities, they may be treated as implicit weights that define the most important components of national power from the perspective of the intelligence community.

Chapter Five

MEASURING NATIONAL RESOURCES

TECHNOLOGY

If the most defining characteristic of the postindustrial age is the emergence of societies "organized around knowledge for the purpose of social control and the directing of innovation and change,"[1] it should not be surprising to find technology—understood as the material instantiation of knowledge, methods, resources, and innovation—identified as the first and most important building block for the production of national power. The number of technologies possessed by a country at any given point in time are not only vast and beyond enumeration, they also span the spectrum of sophistication, ranging from primitive implements all the way to the most cutting-edge products, which can be generated only as a result of attaining mastery over advanced scientific concepts and having both the resources and the ability to translate these concepts, first, into new components and, thereafter, into a larger socio-technical system built around the introduction of these new components. The focus on technology here, as a building block of national power, is centered exclusively on understanding a country's ability to produce the most sophisticated "critical technologies" identified today. The issue of "what is a critical technology" is itself a complex and much debated question, and it cannot be either addressed or resolved in this monograph.[2] There is, however, a loose consensus in govern-

---

[1]Bell, op. cit., p. 20.

[2]An excellent discussion of this question may be found in Bruce A. Bimber and Steven W. Popper, *What Is a Critical Technology?* (Santa Monica, CA: RAND, DRU-605-CTI, 1994). See also Popper et al., op. cit. (1998), pp. 125–133.

ment, industry, and among technologists on which technologies today are deemed to be critical; the National Critical Technologies Panel, for example, has identified 22 separate critical technologies that will be vital to both economic competitiveness and defense in the future.[3] Any evidence of mastery (or of growing capability) in these areas would not only suggest that the target country is likely to be (if it is not already) a contender of significance in the struggles to dominate the cycles of innovation in the international economy but also that it has (or is attempting to create) the technological capabilities to produce instruments of coercion that could proffer an edge in the jostling common to international politics.

Analyzing the Technological Capabilities of a Target Country

Since this remains the analytical focus of the framework suggested in this report, the technological capabilities of any target country ought to be scrutinized at three levels:

The first level is the country's capacity to produce the most important critical technology *today*. Since by common consensus the most important technology today appears to be information and communication technology in all its manifold guises, and since it is also acknowledged that the United States today has the lead in this area, scrutinizing the capacity of key target countries here is intended to disclose whether they are enhancing their capabilities as a result of diffusion, imitation, or innovations of their own. This evidence speaks primarily to whether potential competitors may be catching up with the United States in an arena where it already dominates.

The second level is the country's capacity to produce the most important critical technologies of *tomorrow*. Even as the analysis continues of how competitors may be catching up with the United States in the critical technologies of today, it is important to examine whether competitors are making breakthroughs in other technology-areas that are currently assessed as harboring the potential to transform into the "leading sectors" of tomorrow: materials, manufacturing, biotechnology, aeronautics and surface transportation, and

---

[3]U.S. Department of Commerce, *Report of the National Critical Technologies Panel* (Washington, D.C.: U.S. Government Printing Office, 1991).

energy and environment. Scrutinizing the capacity of key target countries here is intended to disclose whether they are enhancing their capabilities to challenge the economic primacy of the United States as a result of independent, pathbreaking innovations of their own in new technology-areas that could become the nucleus of new leading sectors tomorrow. Since it is never possible to determine conclusively in advance which technology-areas will remain critical for the production of future national power, observers ought to recognize that the candidate critical technologies of tomorrow may change if "new feats . . .[which] . . . initiate an uprush in another industry"[4] ever occur in the United States or abroad. If such "feats" occur, the analytical focus ought to change accordingly. Since the current consensus appears to be that innovations in materials, manufacturing, biotechnology, aeronautics and surface transportation, and energy and environment hold the promise of producing the new leading sectors of tomorrow, the analysis here will focus primarily on these technology-areas even as it reiterates the argument that these currently salient areas could well be replaced by others over time.

The third level is the country's capacity to produce the most important militarily-critical technologies of today. Since technological innovations are usually translated into militarily-relevant instruments by all candidate great powers, the analysis of technology as a building block of national power must include, finally, the scrutiny of a country's ability to produce all the militarily critical technologies deemed to be vital today. These technologies will not be listed in this section, since they are large in number but, more importantly, are described elsewhere in some detail.[5] The authoritative U.S. study of militarily critical technologies has identified about 2,060 militarily significant technologies, of which fully 656 were deemed to be critical for the purposes of developing advanced weaponry, all of which fell within eighteen broad technology areas which, in turn, are further divided into eighty-four subsections.[6] Two considerations are relevant in this regard: First, the militarily-critical technologies

---

[4]Simon S. Kuznets, "Schumpeter's Business Cycles," *American Economic Review*, Vol. 30, No. 2 (1940), pp. 257–271.

[5]Office of the Under Secretary of Defense for Acquisition, *The Militarily Critical Technologies List* (Washington, D.C.: U.S. Government Printing Office, 1992).

[6]Ibid.

identified here span the technologies relevant for the production of leading-edge military instruments both today and, to some degree, tomorrow. Second, this list cannot be considered as cast in stone: the relevant militarily critical technologies will change over time depending on the innovations that occur in the overall national economic base. Consequently, observers must recognize that these technologies are identified on the basis of present estimations of what is possible, and as new technological breakthroughs occur in the wider economy, the range of technologies that lend themselves to critical military applications will also change *pari passu*.

Indicators of Critical Technologies

Information and communications. In an age defined by dramatic advances in information processing, it should not be surprising to find that information and communications have become the new leading sector of the global economy and, by implication, a good metric for judging national power. The number and kinds of technologies encompassed by the notion of an information technology network are vast and diverse, but the most important are those which refer to the critical computing and connectivity technologies that not only "transform . . . economic and social life in ways that hardly need elaboration"[7] but can also be "used to create still better technology."[8] The 1991 Report of the Critical Technologies Panel lists seven separate areas of knowledge necessary to achieve technological excellence in this regard: high-performance computing and networking, software, data storage and peripherals, computer simulation and modeling, microelectronics and optoelectronics, sensors and signal processing, and high-definition imaging and displays.[9]

High-performance computing and networking technologies are essential to the capability to process, store, and transmit information. These technologies provide the ability to manipulate, analyze, compute, and otherwise use information more accurately and quickly than the unaided human brain can. Computing technologies also

[7]Cohen, op. cit., pp. 42–43.

[8]Goure, op. cit., p. 177.

[9]U.S. Department of Commerce, op. cit.

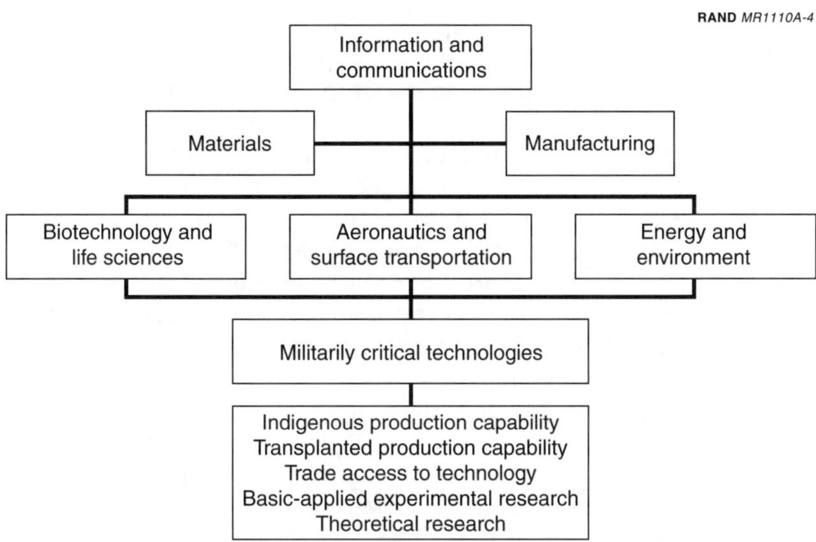

Figure 4—Critical Technologies and Illustrative Indicators

permit the storage of information in accessible forms. High computing performance is indicated by a large magnitude of computational power (the number of calculations in a given unit of time), a large input/output bandwidth (the number of information bits a computer can take in or produce in a unit of time), a high capacity to accommodate different kinds of software, and large storage capacity. Networking technology represents the complement to high-speed computing. It provides the capability to link computers as well as data, image, and voice communications by converting streams of binary data into acoustic, electronic, or photonic signals and vice versa. High-quality networking technology is indicated by the extent of bandwidth (higher bandwidths carry larger numbers of signals per unit time), the quality of transmission, the speed at which signals are processed and transmitted, and the security of the transmissions. Networking also contributes to speedier computing insofar as parallel processing by multiple linked computers results in faster problem solving, which may also obviate the need for gigantic single processors.

Computing capabilities are supported by software and data storage and peripherals technologies. Software provides the basis for applications that allow individuals to direct the physical hardware represented by the computer. Without software programs, computers would be unable to function and users could not interact with them. The quality of software can be judged by its level of sophistication (the complexity, or number of tasks it can accommodate smoothly), its diversity (the range of tasks), and by the flexibility of its program design (the ability of the program to accommodate unanticipated tasks). Software quality can also be assessed negatively, according to the presence of flaws in programming which might cause it to function deviantly. Data storage and peripherals provide the ability to interface physically with computers. Peripherals allow the entering, viewing, manipulation, and storage of data; they include such devices as CD-ROMs (compact disk, read-only memory), floppy disks, keyboards, mice, printers, and scanners. Their quality is best judged by their reliability.

The varied technologies of advanced computing provide the base for simulation and modeling technologies that construct artificial models of processes, actions, interactions, plans, or objects by utilizing high-level computer software and high-speed processors and enormous data storage, access, and retrieval capabilities at the hardware level. By allowing sophisticated, varied-condition testing of anything from completed systems to design prototypes to command methodologies, simulation and modeling technologies facilitate optimal planning and production, which contribute significantly to increasing innovation and efficiency while reducing risks. The adaptability, accuracy, and realism of simulations and models represent their measure of quality.

While the computational technologies identified above certainly represent critical components, the real distinctiveness of the postindustrial age derives from the connectivity of these components, which has enabled the creation of vast integrated systems than can control everything from banking to transportation. Computing technologies thus represent the muscle for manipulating, generating, and storing information, while communications technologies represent the nervous system that supports information and allows it to move from place to place. The most important communications technologies are those of microelectronics and optoelectronics. These technologies provide an ever-increasing capacity to process, disperse, and transmit information. Microelectronics employ microscopic electronic elements—semiconductors—which allow increasing miniaturization and integration of computing power at low cost. Optoelectronics emit, modify, utilize, and/or respond to optical radiation to augment conventional microelectronics. The most prominent development here is laser technology, which can be used as a highly precise cutting tool as well as an instrument for sensing and transmitting information and for guidance. Laser and other optoelectronic technologies have significant applications for industrial processing, telecommunications, computing, surveillance, guided weaponry, medicine, signal processing, and imaging. The best indicators identifying the quality of a country's microelectronics and optoelectronic systems include their operating speeds, reliability, power, efficiency, longevity, and cost.

Two specific applications of microelectronic and optoelectronic technologies merit consideration as critical technologies in their own right: sensor and signal processing technology and high-definition imaging and display technology. Sensor technologies employ microelectronic devices to monitor and/or observe changes in their environment, while signal processing technologies transform the sensors' electrical signals into usable information and transmit it to users. Together these two technologies enable automated systems to interact with the external world. The quality of sensor capabilities can be measured by the accuracy, reliability, and responsiveness of the sensors. Redundancy is also a key quality in a sensor array, since it may correct for localized flaws in the first three areas. The quality of signal processing is indicated by the system's ability to discern between false and true signals, eliminate irrelevant noise, and produce accurate readings.

High-definition imaging and display technology provides the capacity to record and display images with high accuracy, clarity, and speed. This technology relies on capacity for real-time signal processing, high-rate data transmission, and data storage to enable a new level of sophistication in communicating information. Its best-known application is in high-definition television (HDTV), which can be used beyond entertainment for electronic imaging and document storage, digital photocopying, desktop publishing, industrial inspection and monitoring, and battlefield command and control. The quality of high-definition imaging and displays can be determined from the resolution of the image, the quality of the picture, and the speed and efficiency of imaging transmission.

Although attention is properly focused on the criticality of information technology as the key to national, and military, power today, other technological inputs already play a crucial role and may well play an even more important role in the 21st century for the production of material power. They are described below.

Materials. Critical technologies in this category are those pertaining to materials synthesis/processing, electronic and photonic materials, ceramics, composites, and high-performance metals and alloys.

Advances in materials synthesis and processing make it increasingly possible to fashion new materials—atom by atom—to achieve a desired set of properties. The ability to synthesize new materials is central to technological progress in such vital industrial areas as microelectronics, aerospace, transportation, and energy.

The development of electronic and photonic materials is crucial for communications, image processing, and information processing. The key electronic material today is semiconductors. Silicon has, to date, been the dominant material in the manufacture of semiconductors. But future semiconductors made from the GaAs (gallium arsenide) compound offer the prospect of enhanced performance (leading to a new generation of supercomputers), and resistance to nuclear radiation (crucial for both military and space applications). Photonic materials are those that generate, detect, or transmit coherent light, including technologies such as lasers and fiber optic communications.

Advanced, high-performance ceramics have important high-temperature applications, and they also are used in applications that require the capacity to withstand extreme wear or corrosion. In aerospace, the heat-resisting properties of lighter-weight ceramics will be incorporated into the turbines of the next generation of jet engines, thereby increasing performance over the current generation of propulsion systems using heavier superalloys. Ceramics also are important for space vehicles, and they are used in the armor of AFVs. Ceramic components are also increasingly used in advanced automobile engines, semiconductors, and advanced cutting tools.

Ceramics also have potential as wear parts (high-performance aerospace bearings, seals, valves, nozzles, etc.).

Composites are materials hybrids comprised of reinforcing fibers or particles embedded in a matrix. The matrix and reinforcements combine to create a material with properties that are more useful collectively than those of the individual elements. Composites include polymer matrix composites, ceramic matrix composites, metal matrix composites, and carbon-carbon composites. Composites are integral to the manufacture of high-performance military aircraft, other defense systems (helicopters, missiles, AFVs), and space vehicles. Composites are becoming increasingly important in both civilian aircraft manufacturing and automobile manufacturing.

High-performance metals (including alloys) are stronger, stiffer, and more heat resistant than traditional structural metals (such as steel). High-performance metals and alloys are crucially important in the advanced aerospace sector.

Manufacturing. Critical technologies in this category are flexible computer integrated manufacturing, intelligent processing equipment, micro- and nanofabrication, and systems management technologies.

Flexible computer integrated manufacturing integrates product, process, and manufacturing into a single interactive network. It encompasses all aspects of manufacturing, including product engineering and design, production scheduling, part production, product assembly, subcontractor and vendor activities, inspection, and customer service. Flexible computer integrated manufacturing is important not because of its impact on any one product, but because it enhances the efficiency of a nation's overall manufacturing industry across sectors. It is vital to economic growth and competitiveness in today's globalized economy.

Intelligent processing equipment is the foundation on the factory floor upon which advanced manufacturing capabilities are based. Intelligent processing equipment includes robotics, sensors, and controls. Intelligent processing equipment is used across a wide spectrum of manufacturing activities, including machining, forming, welding, heat treating, composite fabricating, painting, testing, inspecting, and material handling. State-of-the-art intelligent processing equipment is especially critical to maintaining competitive manufacturing capabilities, especially in high-technology sectors.

Micro- and nanofabrication involve the manipulation of materials at the microscopic, and atomic, levels respectively. Micro- and nanofabrication processes are essential in producing semiconductors. Microfabrication processes include lithography, etching, disposition, diffusion, implantation, and packaging. Other expected applications involve high-density integrated circuits, optoelectronic devices, quantum devices, and textured surfaces for biotechnology. Semiconductors and integrated circuits are, of course, at the core of the information and communications technologies. As such, they have important "downstream" effects on a state's economy and on its military capabilities. Micro- and nanofabrication are crucial to attaining leading-edge capabilities in semiconductors and integrated circuits.

Systems management technologies are information technologies that allow implementation of advanced systems management concepts. They include product exchange tools, databases, data-driven management information systems, and interoperable information systems. Application of systems management technologies is crucial to attainment of leading-edge capabilities in manufacturing.

Biotechnology and life sciences. This category includes applied molecular biology, which is based on recombinant DNA technology, protein engineering, monoclonal antibody production, and bioprocessing. Recombinant DNA has fueled the creation of important therapeutic and preventive proteins, including vaccines, human insulin, human growth hormone, cancer-fighting agents, and drugs for blood disorders. Recombinant DNA technology also promises to lead to the development of gene therapy that will be able to prevent, or treat, inherited diseases. Recombinant DNA technology also has applications in areas such as agriculture and food processing. Protein engineering has important industrial applications, and it also has implications for the development of new therapeutic drugs. Monoclonal antibody production allows the development of specialized antibodies able to attack only a specific disease-causing agent or cell type. Monoclonal antibodies are used to treat cancer, HIV, and cystic fibrosis. They may also lead to the development of highly sensitive detection systems for plant and animal diseases, as well as food-borne pathogens. Bioprocessing is the link between biotechnological science and the production of drugs, food enzymes and ingredients, and specialty products for industry and agriculture. Applied molecular biology is an important leading-edge technology that affects health/disease prevention, agriculture, and environmental regulation (fabrication of enzymes that degrade solid waste and toxic chemicals or clean up oil spills).

Aeronautics and surface transportation. Aeronautics embraces a diverse array of technologies that are key to the design, development, production, performance, and safety of aircraft. In terms of state power, the important technologies are those utilized by advanced aircraft, including large subsonic transports, high-performance military aircraft (both fixed and rotary wing), and supersonic and hypersonic aircraft. Key technological areas include propulsion, aviation materials and structures, aerodynamics, human factors engineering, aircraft manufacturing, and aeronautical testing. The importance of aeronautics as a component of state power is obvious: advanced military aircraft remain on the leading edge of technology. Moreover, aeronautics has feedback interactions with other key technological sectors, including information, electronics, and manufacturing.

Surface transportation technologies include attempts to create intelligent vehicle and highway systems that will use advanced technology to increase driver safety, increase system capacity, and reduce emissions, fuel consumption, and congestion. Also included in surface transportation technologies are various approaches to developing more energy-efficient vehicles, including those that rely on energy sources other than fossil fuels. Surface transportation technologies will enable states to upgrade their transportation infrastructures, which are vital to overall economic growth. Increases in fuel efficiency and development of alternative propulsion sources hold out the prospect of freeing the state from dependence on fossil fuels extracted from geopolitically unstable areas like the Persian Gulf.

Energy and environment. The present reliance of advanced industrial states, as well as newly industrializing states, on fossil fuels as a primary energy source raises both geopolitical and environmental issues.[10] There are two broad technological approaches to meeting these problems. The first is the quest to develop renewable energy sources, including solar thermal power, wind turbines, photovoltaics, and biomass/alternative fuels. A second approach is to develop technologies that allow existing fuel sources to be utilized in a way that minimizes environmental damage. For example, improvements in combustion and catalytic processes could enable coal to be used without adverse economic effects. Advances are also being pursued in nuclear fission technology to make it safer and more reliable by employing light-water, gas-cooled, and liquid metal reactors. Technologies that enhance energy conservation are also important, as are advances in energy storage such as fuel cells and batteries. Energy and environmental technologies will be a vital component of state power. Not only are fossil fuel supplies finite, they force states to rely on suppliers in politically volatile regions. For states, energy security and economic growth in the future demand that advanced technology create new energy sources.

Assessing a country's technology base clearly requires an assessment of its capabilities in each of the six areas identified above. Assessing its militarily-critical technology base requires an assessment of the eighteen broad technology areas mentioned earlier—work that is already under way within the U.S. government. In each of these areas, an adequate assessment requires information about a country's skills at five levels: (i) whether a country has indigenous production capabilities in the technology area; (ii) whether a country has transplanted production capabilities deriving from its status as a host for foreign-owned facilities; (iii) whether a country has trade access to foreign capabilities in a given technology area; (iv) whether a country engages in basic and applied research and developmental work, even if not in commercial production; and (v) whether a country undertakes theoretical research in the technology area in question.

While the list of technologies identified here is neither precise nor exhaustive, it is nonetheless intended to indicate that *science-driven*

---

[10]For the argument that China's continued growth could lead to increased geostrategic rivalry with South Korea, Japan, the United States, and the so-called South east Asian tigers for control of Middle East oil, see Kent E. Calder, *Pacific Defense* (Princeton: Princeton University Press, 1996).

capabilities constitute the first and among the most important kinds of resources in the postindustrial age. Because science and technology persists as a driver of change in modern civilization, the level of technology existing in a given country—especially insofar as it is manifested in cutting-edge instruments that exploit information technology today and other kinds of sophisticated technologies tomorrow—can be ignored only at our peril. No matter how sophisticated a country's technology actually is, however, it does not exist in a vacuum. Its existence is often the product of complex—prior—societal and state choices, so any assessment of a country's technological resources must inevitably shift its focus beyond a point from the concrete artifacts concerned to the entrepreneurial capabilities that produced them.

ENTERPRISE

Although the concept of "enterprise" usually has many shades of meaning, depending on the context in which it is used, we define it here as a collective expression for the level of invention, innovation, and the diffusion of innovation within a given society. Viewed in this way, enterprise is understood as the natural progenitor of technology in that it refers to the societal dimensions of capability that make technology—the critical engines of power in the postindustrial age—possible. By incorporating the notion of enterprise as a component of national power, this framework seeks to emphasize that technology does not subsist autonomously but is always a product of prior societal and state choices in other areas like education and health, investments in human capital, and communications and infrastructure. While this fact cannot be ignored, the quality of entrepreneurial capabilities nonetheless remains an *immediately* important variable because it provides a country with the only means of overcoming the scarcities inherent in nature. Since capital and labor are essentially limited, national growth would inevitably hit a ceiling as a country progressively exhausts its finite pool of resources. This outcome of stagnation and, eventually, decay—the nightmare of classical economics—can be arrested only by technological progress, which at its core consists of nothing other than new and better ways to use existing resources. The ability to generate technological

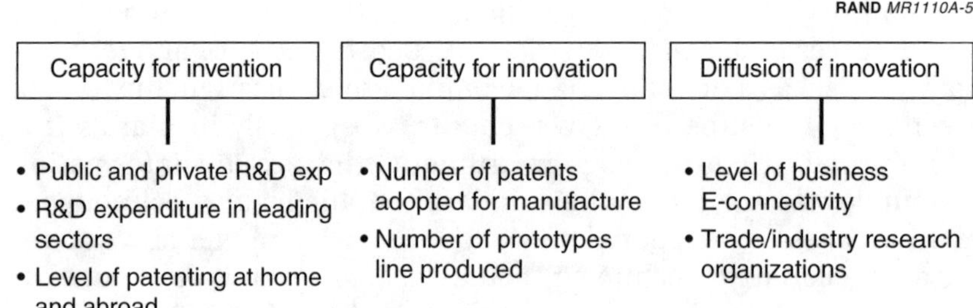

Figure 5—Entrepreneurship and Illustrative Indicators

progress is, in turn, a function of the entrepreneurial capacity of a society that is very often both stimulated and directed as a result of deliberate state choices. Irrespective of what the source of such entrepreneurship may be, the capacity to invent, innovate, and diffuse innovations is critical because it creates a multiplier effect that serves to overcome many of the disadvantages of a limited, even poor, natural resource endowment.

Indicators of Entrepreneurship

Assessing a country's level of entrepreneurship as a component of its national power, then, requires a systematic scrutiny of both its potential and actual capability to invent, innovate, and diffuse its innovations, and each of these three dimensions, which were first elaborated by Schumpeter in 1912,[11] will be briefly described in turn.

Capacity for invention. The concept of invention generally refers to the advancement of any new idea, sketch, or model for a new or improved product, process, or system. Invention in this sense does not necessarily imply demonstrating the feasibility of the new product or process, or even the creation of a prototype, but it must embody a reasoned justification that the idea or model proposed will actually work and often includes some preliminary test to demon-

---

[11]J. A. Schumpeter, *The Theory of Economic Development* (Cambridge: Harvard University Press, 1934).

strate that it actually does.[12] What exactly the sources of invention are is an interesting, but difficult, question to answer. Clearly, the stock of scientific knowledge possessed by a society at any given moment in time is a crucial factor, since this knowledge provides the base from which all inventions come. However, human creativity, inspiration, and genius all play a vital role as well, though these are by definition the idiosyncratic elements of the process. The causes of any given invention, therefore, are many and varied: invention may simply be a chance event characterized in fact by many prior failures; it may be the result of the superior knowledge and abilities of certain inventors; given the necessary background knowledge, it may arise from sufficient and appropriate private and public investment in science and technological activity; or it may be rooted ultimately in economic incentives, often provided by the state, that are aimed at producing specific scientific discoveries and inventions.[13] Early studies seemed to suggest that individual inventors and small firms played a significant role where inventions were concerned, but whether this is true even today, when large-scale private and public investments in basic and applied research are often necessary for the creation of new products and processes, is unclear.[14]

In any event, assessing a country's capacity to produce useful inventions, especially in the core technology areas identified in the last subsection, may be captured by a variety of measures. To begin with, the levels of investment in research and development provide a useful first cut that depicts how seriously a country pursues the benefits of technical change. Government expenditures on R&D as a percentage of GNP are a particularly important index because studies suggest that the annual rate of return from R&D to society as a whole may be close to 50 percent, a value assessed to be twice the private return to an individual firm.[15] The level of government R&D expenditures in the core technology areas identified previously rep-

[12]J. Jewkes, D. Sawers, and R. Stillerman, *The Sources of Invention* (London: Macmillan, 1958).

[13]P. Stoneman, *The Economic Analysis of Technological Change* (New York: Oxford University Press, 1983).

[14]Jewkes, Sawers, and Stillerman, op. cit.

[15]Pam Woodall, "The World Economy: The Hitchhiker's Guide to Cybernomics," *The Economist*, September 28, 1996, p. 44.

resents another more focused measure of inventive potential. Government-level expenditures alone, however, may not be sufficient to assess the potential for invention because these values are crucially affected by the character of state-society relations within a given country. Strong states presumably will spend more on R&D (both generally and in specific technology areas) than weak states might, but strong societies may in some instances spend as much if not more on R&D both generally and specifically in comparison to some strong states. Consequently, aggregate private R&D expenditures as a function of GNP, as well as more focused expenditures on critical technology, should also be assessed as a complementary measure of the inventive potential of a country.

Where actual inventive performance is concerned, however, patenting activity appears to provide the best measure of national inventiveness.[16] Examining the record of patents applied for and secured helps to assess the productivity of a country's resident inventors and by implication may even provide an intuitive measure of the quality of a country's education and science and technology (S&T) base. The first specific measure that might be appropriate for measuring a country's actual inventiveness therefore consists simply of identifying the level of domestic patenting activity both generally and in the specific technology areas mentioned previously.[17] But because patenting systems and the laws governing intellectual property rights vary across countries, a useful complementary measure of inventiveness consists of measuring not just domestic patenting but patents actually sought and secured by inventors in foreign countries, especially the United States. Patenting in the United States is actually an appropriate numeraire for assessing the inventiveness of all other countries, since the United States not only has an excellent and well-organized patent office but is also the wealthiest country, whose

[16]An excellent analysis of patenting as a measure of inventiveness can be found in Z.Griliches, "Patent Statistics as Economic Indicators: A Survey," *Journal of Economic Literature,* Vol. 28, No. 4 (December 1990), pp. 1661–1707.

[17]Since patenting can also reflect activity associated with foreign licensed production in a given country, however, information about the *origins* of the product or processes patented would be a useful corrective to aggregate data on patent activity. Information about the origins of a new product or process is usually available to patent examiners in every case, but it is unclear whether aggregate data identifying the origins of patented products or processes are available.

vibrant economic system attracts leading-edge technologies that foreign inventors would seek to protect for purposes of revenue generation both in the United States and abroad.[18] These foreign patents secured within the United States should again be measured in aggregate terms as well as in disaggregated form, focusing on activity in the high-technology fields identified earlier.

Capacity for innovation. While inventiveness certainly remains at the root of technical change in any society, it is but one element in the larger measurement of enterprise as a variable in national power. For inventions to become valuable they must be transformed eventually into innovations, or else they remain merely novel ideas of no economic consequence. Schumpeter, insistently pointing to the distinction between invention and innovation, used the latter concept to structure his entire theory of economic development insofar as he posited the entrepreneur-as-innovator to be the prime mover of all technological change. The Schumpeterian emphasis on innovation is critical because while inventions may occur idiosyncratically at various places and times, the ability to innovate—which includes the issue of receptivity to other people's inventions and creations—provides the motive force that transforms the existing economic and technological order. Innovation in this context is defined not simply as the generation of a new idea or product but rather the *first introduction of a new product, process, method, or system into the national economy.* The process of innovation thus refers to the development or the exploitation of an invention insofar as it is actually used or produced as an economic good within the economy, and here Schumpeter distinguished between five kinds of innovations: the introduction of a new good (or dramatic improvements in the quality of existing goods), the introduction of new methods of production, the opening of new markets, the securing of new sources of supply of raw materials or intermediate goods, and the creation of new forms of industrial organization. Schumpeter used this typology to indicate that the innovator was, therefore, necessarily neither the inventor of a product nor the risk-bearer, since risk-bearing remains the provenance of the capitalist who advances the requisite funds to the innovator.

---

[18]K. Pavitt, "Patent Statistics as Indicators of Innovative Activities: Possibilities and Problems," *Scientometrics,* Vol. 7 (1985), pp. 77–99.

The innovator thus remains "merely" a decisionmaker, but one whose attentiveness to the potential profitability of new inventions and whose willingness to make judgments about product choices in the face of uncertainty makes him a critical element in the process by which new ideas, methods, and goods actually reach the marketplace and, thereby, become valuable commodities which can eventually contribute to a country's national power. Because innovation hinges on risky judgments about a product's potential economic value and because transforming an invention into a marketable commodity may require the application of great resources—due in part to the problems of scaling laboratory products for mass production and debugging inventions of potential defects prior to mass manufacture—it is not surprising to find fewer innovators than inventors in any society. In part, this is simply because although most inventions are patented, few ever make it to commercial production, since many, if not most, patents are used primarily as bargaining counters for the sake of revenue sharing.[19]

Schumpeter himself argued that because of the complexity, cost, and risks attending any efforts at innovation, large firms—enjoying the benefits of size and possibly other monopolies—would be advantaged in the struggle to innovate. Since the publication of his work in 1934, this claim has provoked a good deal of debate and dissension, and while important new insights have been gained into what accounts for the success and failure of private efforts at innovation, it is still unclear as to which government policies are more likely to encourage national innovation and promote eventual economic success. Rothwell and Zegveld correctly argue that this uncertainty arises mainly because it is difficult to isolate any single measure like a tax incentive, development subsidy, or procurement initiative from the more general economic influences on the behavior of the firm and the numerous factors which may be specific to any individual firm.[20] These difficulties, unfortunately, impose certain limitations on how a country's potential capacity to innovate may be evaluated, but at least two measures relating to the actual level of innovation suggest themselves: compiling data relating to the number of prod-

[19]C. Freeman, *The Economics of Industrial Innovation* (Cambridge: MIT Press, 1982).

[20]R. R. Rothwell and W. Zegveld, *Industrial Innovation and Public Policy* (London: Frances Pinter, 1981).

uct or process patents adopted for manufacture and the percentage of prototypes actually line produced either across the economy as a whole or within the critical technology areas identified earlier. Either or both of these measures would help to indicate the level of innovation witnessed within a given country and thereby contribute to a qualitative assessment of the entrepreneurial capacity exhibited within the country as a whole.

Diffusion of innovation. The third and last dimension of enterprise measures focuses on the diffusion of innovations within a productive system. This dimension is crucial for the creation of national power because the diffusion of innovations—be they products or processes—represents the process by which productivity gains can be dispersed throughout society at large. Because new production techniques as well as products can be imitated by firms other than their creators, it is possible for goods and services not only to be produced at lower costs but also in an expanded variety and range. Moreover, the diffusion of such artifacts could lead to further invention and innovation insofar as the emergence of a single product, especially in a competitive market system, often gives rise to competitive efforts at either improvement or substitution, as well as to the creation of other complementary products that increase the value of the original good. The diffusion of innovations is thus critical because, by bringing in its wake a multiplier effect, it ensures the dissemination of technical change throughout the economy, helping to offset the limitations imposed by the natural scarce supply of capital and labor.

To be sure, the process of diffusion is often difficult to trace out because the innovated products are often altered as they are disseminated throughout the economy. Yet it is important to try to capture this dimension of enterprise, because several studies have convincingly demonstrated that the technological distinctiveness of innovations more than any other variable (like price distinctiveness, for example) accounts for a country's comparative advantage in the international economic system.[21] The ability to diffuse innovations

---

[21]This finding was first demonstrated in 1966 by Gary Hufbauer in his study, *Synthetic Materials and the Theory of International Trade* (London: Duckworth, 1966), where it was shown that innovation in the production of synthetic materials increased the comparative advantage of producers more than other variables, like price or factor

effectively must therefore be seen as deriving from two broad but different kinds of sources. The first source, which must be tapped as a measure of diffusive capacity, is simply the degree of connectivity of different firms with the rest of the national economy. Connectivity is a good indicator of a firm's capacity to exchange information and ideas, attract customers, advertise products, and eventually spawn competition as well as improvements to its product line. Furthermore, connectivity is also a prerequisite for businesses to be able to exploit information and data in their competition for market share. A simple indicator of connectivity would consist of data relating to (i) the percentage of businesses either throughout the economy or in the critical technology sectors specified earlier that use electronic mail, have their own Web pages, and advertise on the World Wide Web; and (ii) the volume of e-business as a percentage of total business within the economy. A second indicator in this regard might simply be the usage of information technologies within a given country measured by the number of computers, Internet connections and bandwith, and communication devices available per 1,000 individuals.

The second source, which must be tapped as a measure of diffusive capacity, is the number of specialized national or industrywide research institutes that play a role in building up cumulative technological capability. Because evidence suggests that technical know-how, skills, and innovative capacity do account for the differences in national economic performance,[22] the number of national or industrywide research institutes existing in a country provides a good insight into how well a given society can disseminate technical knowledge in order to secure the multiplier effects that stem from innovation at large. It has, for example, been cogently argued that German advantages in the chemical and engineering industries have been related to the "Technische Hochschulen" set up since the 19th century, and that Japanese excellence more recently also owes its robustness to similar institutions.

---

proportions, which were deemed to be important by standard models like the Heckscher-Olin theory of trade.

[22]See, by way of example, K.L.R. Pavitt, *Technical Innovation and British Economic Performance* (London: Macmillan, 1980).

Enterprise, understood as the capacity to invent, innovate, and diffuse innovations, thus remains the motor of technological change. The ability to promote and sustain rapid technological change, in turn, functions as the foundation upon which national power is built. The discussion above clearly suggests that enterprise, like technology, does not exist as a natural building block of national power. Rather, it emerges from within the human capital stock of a given society, since the ability to invent, innovate, and diffuse innovations is little other than an extended product of the national investments—both private and state sponsored—made in human resources. The next section, therefore, examines human resources as an independent building block of national power.

HUMAN RESOURCES

While the most visible elements of the postindustrial age are the myriad information technologies visible throughout society, the most critical component of this era—though manifested in technology and the innovations that give rise to it—is the individuals who create its various artifacts. Since knowledge has become the new "axial principle"[23] on which the postindustrial age is built, the resources invested in human beings for the creation, codification, and assimilation of knowledge become critical not only for the maintenance of a given society but also for the production of national power and political control. A sophisticated framework for measuring national capabilities must therefore concentrate on assessing the productive capacities of human beings as income-, wealth-, and technology-producing agents precisely because the production of actionable knowledge, including that which eventually enables the efficient creation and employment of an effective military force, constitutes the foundation on which national power is built today.

In some sense, the insight that human resources are important for national power is not new. It dates back to Adam Smith, who argued in *The Wealth of Nations* that the improvement of workers' skills constituted the main source of economic progress and increased economic welfare. In the same work, Smith in fact demonstrated

---

[23]Bell, op. cit., p. 20.

how investments in human capital not only affect an individual's personal income but also transform the structure of wages in the marketplace. Almost a century and a half later, Frank Knight contended that investments in human capital were the key to improving a society's stock of productive knowledge in order to stave off the effects of diminishing returns in a growing economy.[24] The basic ideas about the relationship between human capital and economic growth were thus understood and recognized by economists for a long time, but the decisive demonstration of the importance of human resources came only in the 1950s and 1960s, when the availability of detailed national income data revealed that aggregate national output grew at a more rapid pace than aggregate factor inputs. Although many explanations for this divergence had in fact been offered, the most persuasive hypothesis seems to have been the presence of hitherto unexplained technical change, and it fell to Theodore Schultz and Edward Denison to explicate how "human capital"—meaning the secular improvements in worker skills as a function of education, training, and literacy—accounted for the improved quality of factor inputs which, in turn, resulted in the disproportionate increase seen in aggregate output.[25]

The recognition that investments in human capital have disproportionate effectiveness, thus, predates the postindustrial age. But at a time when economic growth and national power are increasingly driven by the ability to create and apply the "actionable knowledge" that produces high-technology and higher-value-added products, investments in human capital take on a specific coloration and meaning. Because knowledge per se is not scarce in the traditional sense of the term—that is, its quantity diminishes as it is used—but the ability to understand and use knowledge certainly is—in that not all individuals can use a society's knowledge base with equal skill and dexterity, not to mention contribute by expanding it—any useful measure of national power must focus its attention primarily on those kinds of human capital which concern "the directing of inno-

[24]F. Knight, "Diminishing Returns from Investment," *Journal of Political Economy*, Vol. 52 (March 1944), pp. 26–47.

[25]T. Schultz, "Investment in Human Capital," *American Economic Review*, Vol. 51 (March 1961), pp. 1–17, and E. Denison, *The Sources of Economic Growth in the United States and the Alternatives Before Us* (New York: Committee for Economic Development, 1962).

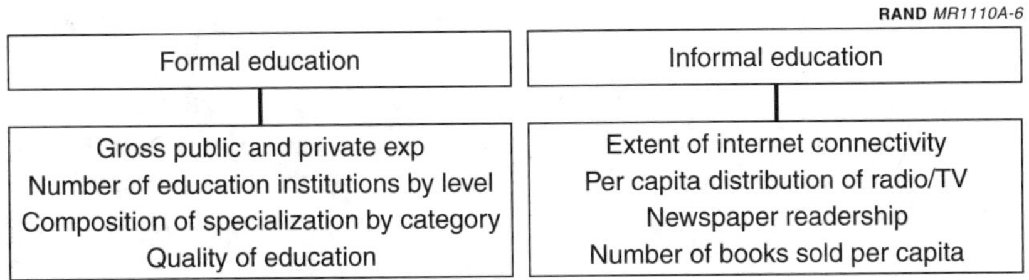

Figure 6—Human Resources and Illustrative Indicators

vation and change."[26] In other words, they must measure the human capital that, relating directly to the acquisition, codification, and application of scientific knowledge, not only drives the specific character of the postindustrial age but also increases the skills and productivity of labor both within and across countries.

Indicators of Human Capital Resources

The most general measure of human capital that captures this dimension is a country's expenditure on education and its number of educational institutions. Both education expenditures and the number of institutions—private and public—must be disaggregated to capture the relative emphasis on primary, secondary, tertiary, and vocational and continuing education. Such data convey the importance levied on improving the quality of a country's potential work force, and, to equalize for disparities in the size of population, this information should also be structured on a per-capita basis in addition to data about gross totals. Information of this sort should identify, at least as a first cut, the size of a country's educational infrastructure and the importance placed on fostering knowledge-based strategies for increasing economic growth and national power.

While information about the size and balance of the educational infrastructure is vital, it is not sufficient. It must be supplemented by information about enrollment at all educational levels, with special attention paid to the tertiary level, since the net analytic capacity of the work force will be of a higher caliber in direct proportion to the

[26] Bell, op. cit., p. 20.

percentage of the population that attends university, and higher still according to the percentage that actually receives an associate's, bachelor's, master's, or doctoral degree.[27] With the increasing access to international education, the number of students receiving an education abroad at all levels (but especially the tertiary level) should also be accounted for. An important derivative indicator here would be enrollment and attainment data pertaining to foreign students (especially by area of study) receiving an education in the United States. Assessing the emphasis placed on secondary and more importantly tertiary education is crucial for evaluating a country's capacity to participate in and exploit the postindustrial economy. This is because secondary and tertiary education in particular place a premium on analytic capability: the ability to formulate a problem, gather information, recognize patterns, and synthesize information.[28] These skills become particularly relevant in the knowledge-based economy, where the process of asking the right questions, finding the data necessary to answer those questions, processing that data to create meaningful answers, and synthesizing those answers to create the knowledge required to resolve the initial problem remains the foundation on which the technology invent-and-innovate cycle can proceed uninterruptedly.

The information pertaining to the enrollment in higher education needs to be further refined if it is to capture certain critical dimensions of human capital that are relevant to the postindustrial age. Among the most important such refinements is the composition of specializations among the highly educated subset of the populace. The British historian Correlli Barnett has illustrated the crucial role that the composition of education plays in the production of national power by comparing the very different German and English approaches to higher education at the turn of the century. While England's elite universities stressed a curriculum based on the classics, the Germans stressed science (both pure research and applied science), engineering, and administrative and organizational tech-

[27]The Harbison-Myers Skills Index is one example of such an index that measures the attainments in secondary education and beyond as a measure of national capacity. See The World Bank, *World Development Report 1992* (New York: Oxford University Press, 1993) for its application.

[28]Casey Wardynski, "The Labor Economics of Information Warfare," *Military Review*, Vol. 75, No. 3 (May/June 1995), pp. 56–61.

niques. Reviewing the data, Barnett concluded that to a large extent, the early 20th century contest for economic and, hence, geopolitical supremacy between Germany and Britain "was lost in the school-yards and quadrangles of Britain"[29] long before its effects were ever made manifest in terms of the decline in English power. Measuring human capital as a contributor to national power therefore requires disaggregated information about the composition of specialization in five general areas: mathematics and physical sciences, biological sciences, engineering, social and behavioral sciences, and the arts and humanities. While the last specialization is necessary for the preservation of culture and humanity, it is less relevant in comparison to the first three disciplines for the production of national power; the social and behavioral sciences fall in between. In any event, the data about the composition of specialization should indicate the extent to which a country places a focused emphasis on the production of actionable knowledge pertinent to the postindustrial age.[30]

Finally, the last measure of a country's human capital consists of assessing the quality of a country's system of higher education and the levels of recognized excellence that may exist in its knowledge-production complex, especially in the key areas of mathematics-physical sciences, biological sciences, and engineering. Quality and excellence merit evaluation because they provide an important indicator of a nation's ability to renew its knowledge base and thereby increase its relative power. The objective of the indicators here must be to measure the quality of scholarship and research, the system's effectiveness in training new scholars and researchers, and the extent and value of research productivity. Such assessments are generally difficult to produce, and most traditional efforts in this regard consist almost exclusively of "reputational ratings" derived entirely from peer evaluations.[31] Such ratings are useful, but they are afflicted by multiple difficulties that cannot be easily overlooked.[32]

---

[29]Correlli Barnett, *The Pride and the Fall: The Dream and Illusion of Britain as a Great Nation* (New York: Free Press, 1986), p. 205.

[30]This information would obviously be supplemented by the data relating to enrollment and attainment data of foreign nationals receiving an education in the United States.

[31]The history of reputational assessments in the United States is briefly explored in A. Granbard, "Notes Toward a New History," in J. Cole, E. Barber, and A. Granbard, *The*

For this reason, educational quality, especially between countries, is best compared using a few additional objective criteria, even though these criteria are by no means exhaustive and are in fact quite modest. To begin with, it must be recognized that "there is no single agreed index of a unitary attribute called 'quality' [but only] several 'qualities,' and the importance of them is largely a function of the needs of the [observer]."[33] Further, quality cannot be measured across the education system as a whole but only within disciplinary boundaries; accordingly, the analyst must select those disciplines which are most relevant for the production of power and judge national quality within those specific research areas. And, finally, it is worth remembering that it is always easier to assess quality about the strongest and weakest educational programs, but much more difficult to assess programs in the middle range. Bearing these caveats in mind, there are several objective criteria of educational quality worth exploring as indices of national performance in a given disciplinary area. These include (i) the number of published articles and books emerging from a given research area; (ii) the estimated "overall influence"[34] of published articles and books; (iii) the number of recognized national and international grants awarded to researchers in a given discipline; (iv) the number of recognized awards and honors earned by researchers in a given research area; and (v) the number and quality of advanced research institutes focusing on key science and technology areas of importance to the production of national power.

Research University in a Time of Discontent (Baltimore: Johns Hopkins, 1994), pp. 361–390.

[32]The difficulties of reputational ratings are usefully surveyed in John Shelton Reed, "How Not to Measure What a University Does," *The Chronicle of Higher Education*, Vol. 22, No. 12 (1981), and Lyle V. Jones, Gardner Lindzey, and Porter E. Coggeshall (eds.), *An Assessment of Research-Doctorate Programs in the United States: Mathematical and Physical Sciences* (Washington, D.C.: National Academy Press, 1982), pp. 3–6.

[33]Marvin L. Goldberger, Brendan A. Mahler, and Pamela Ebert Flattau (eds.), *Research-Doctorate Programs in the United States* (Washington, D.C.: National Academy Press, 1995), p. ix.

[34]An elaborate methodology for evaluating "overall influence" has been developed in Francis Narin, *Evaluative Bibliometrics: The Use of Publications and Citations Analysis in the Evaluation of Scientific Activity, Report to the National Science Foundation,* March 1976.

There is no doubt that measuring the quality of a country's human capital stock is a difficult but at the same time necessary undertaking. A comprehensive measure would require accounting for direct improvements in human productive ability not simply through education but also through more remote investments in health and human welfare. Accounting for such remote investments, however, would complicate considerably the measures of national power proposed here, so they are excluded. Besides the practical concerns deriving from the need for parsimony and manageability, such an exclusion can also be justified at the theoretical level on the grounds that it is reasonable to presume that individuals who appear in the educated subset of the population already have minimal access to health care and a hospitable social environment. Thus, concentrating on education not only provides the benefit of focusing on the measure that directly relates to the effectiveness of the work force—which is after all a stock of skills and productive knowledge embodied in people—but it also, arguably, serves as a reasonable proxy for other more remote measures relating to health and welfare. It is also worth recognizing in this connection that more extensive measures about education itself could be supplied for purposes of assessment: these could include, for example, the access of the labor force to retraining and continuing education, the skills and qualifications of managers, and the like. Such measures too have been avoided because they are in some sense implicit in the measures of access to education proposed above and, more important, because the overall skills and training of the population provide a better guide to the quality of a country's human capital than the access to specific kinds of educational opportunity enjoyed by one subgroup or another.

Resources in the form of human capital arguably remain one of the most critical inputs for the production of national power. The quality of this capital is directly responsible for the entrepreneurial character visible in a country, and this in turn creates the technology base that fundamentally affects the national power a country can produce. While human capital is thus further responsible for the production of actionable knowledge, it is—like all the other inputs examined before it—also an artificial building block of national power. That is, it is owed to prior human decisions and in particular to the non-human-capital stocks possessed and created within a country. These non-human-capital stocks, usually subsumed by the locution "economic power," will be examined as one more critical—but artificial—input in the production of national power.

FINANCIAL/CAPITAL RESOURCES

The concept of nonhuman capital occupies a central position in neoclassical theories of production and distribution, but it is nonetheless one of the most hotly contested concepts in modern economics.[35] The conventional definition of capital is that it is a stock of produced commodities essential for production, commodities that are subject, more or less, to wear and tear depending on the extent and the methods of their use. This view embodies an understanding of capital as a stock of "capital goods," that is, a series of heterogeneous goods each having specific technical characteristics. The heterogeneity of capital goods, however, creates particular problems that prevent them from being aggregated in terms of a single uniform yardstick. One solution to this difficulty has taken the form of arguments for better or more appropriate indices to aggregate heterogeneous capital goods in terms of some scalar measure.[36] Another solution, which derives from a distinct tradition in economic analysis dating back to Adam Smith, has been to avoid aggregating capital goods altogether but rather to focus on aggregating their value. Treating capital as a sum of values sidesteps the problem of aggregation, but it does create other problems of its own: by reducing a stock of real goods to a bookkeeping valuation of those assets, it opens the door to the possibility that capital values could change even though the stock of real goods itself remains unaltered. The relationship between real capital goods and their expressed value, even when stated in money terms, therefore remains problematic, though some economists have suggested that real counterparts to capital values can be constructed in principle, though not without difficulty.[37]

---

[35]For a good review of the modern debates about capital, see Mark Blaug, *The Cambridge Revolution: Success or Failure?* (London: Institute of Economic Affairs, 1974), and John R. Hicks, "Capital Controversies, Ancient and Modern," in John R. Hicks, *Economic Perspectives* (Oxford: Clarendon Press, 1977).

[36]D. G. Champernowne, "The Production Function and the Theory of Capital: A Comment," *Review of Economic Studies*, Vol. 21 (1954), pp. 112–135.

[37]Hicks, op. cit., p. 151ff, and H.A.J. Green, p. 120.

Such fundamental disagreements about the notion of capital and how to account for it are only complemented by continuing disputes about whether, and in what sense, capital may be treated as a productive element in economic growth. These debates, while fascinating, cannot be surveyed here, much less resolved, so the notion of capital employed in this analysis is drawn largely from the work of economists like John Clark and Frank Knight *mainly because of its utility for the purpose of assessing national power.* Although Clark clearly distinguished between material capital and capital as a "quantum of productive wealth,"[38] the development of his views by Knight and others over time resulted in capital being depicted essentially as a homogenous mass created by savings decisions, which can be easily transferred from one industry to another. Although consisting ultimately of heterogeneous goods, it came to be visualized as a fund of resources which could be switched between multiple uses and is productive in the sense that "it has a non-negative marginal product if used properly" and "which guarantee[s] higher productivity if employed in larger amounts in relation to other factors of production."[39] This Clark-Knight conception of capital—though highly controversial in economics—has been adopted in some form or another by most political theorists, for example Klaus Knorr, who argued that the importance of wealth or capital for politics derives precisely from its fungibility, that is, its easy convertibility into "virtually all types of power and influence."[40]

While the fungibility of capital may be valuable from a political perspective because it implies a certain flexibility of allocation with respect to power political ends, the value of capital from an economic perspective derives from more fundamental considerations relating to the nature and processes of growth. The desirability of capital here derives primarily from its ability to enhance an economy's capability to satisfy a greater range of human needs than before

---

[38]Clark, p. 119.

[39]K. H. Hennings, "Capital as a Factor of Production," in John Eatwell, Murray Milgate, and Peter Newman (eds.), *Capital Theory: The New Palgrave* (New York: W. W. Norton, 1990), p. 116.

[40]Klaus Knorr, *Power and Wealth* (New York: Basic Books, 1973), p. 75.

and, as A. K. Cairncross explained, it does so in three ways.[41] First, a greater abundance of capital enables the institutionalization of more "roundabout" methods of production. This implies that societies with higher stocks of capital can use more capital instruments in the production of any given good, and this results not only in increased productivity but also in greater consumption and enhanced incomes accruing to a larger range of productive agents in the economy. Second, a greater accumulation of capital enables broader economic expansion than might be possible otherwise. This process is generally referred to widening—as opposed to deepening—the structure of production, and it arises when new productive activities are undertaken as a result of more easily available capital; or when changes in the balance between industries makes additional demands on available resources; or when markets extend as a result of population growth, more favorable terms of trade, or the discovery of natural resources. Third, a greater accretion of capital enables the pursuit of rapid technical change. It finances the discovery of what was unknown before or the adaptation of existing knowledge for purposes of commercial exploitation; it underwrites the costs of restructuring organizational changes as well as provides for investment in new human capital. For all these reasons, capital becomes the principal avenue through which all other determinants, whatever those may be, condition the long-run development and prospects facing a country's power.

Indicators of Financial/Capital Resources

While capital enables growth through the three mechanisms identified in Figure 7, it should be obvious by now that it is not an "original" factor of production (in the sense that uncultivated land and raw labor are usually taken to be), but only an outcome resulting from prior economic activity. Consequently, the processes resulting in the creation of capital take on a special importance from the perspective of producing national power. Here, at least, the simple dynamics of capital accumulation are easy to explain, even if they are difficult to undertake in practice: capital increases by investment,

---

[41]The discussion in this paragraph is drawn from A. K. Cairncross, "The Place of Capital in Economic Progress," in L. H. Dupriez (ed.), *Economic Progress* (Louvain: International Economic Association, 1955), pp. 235–248.

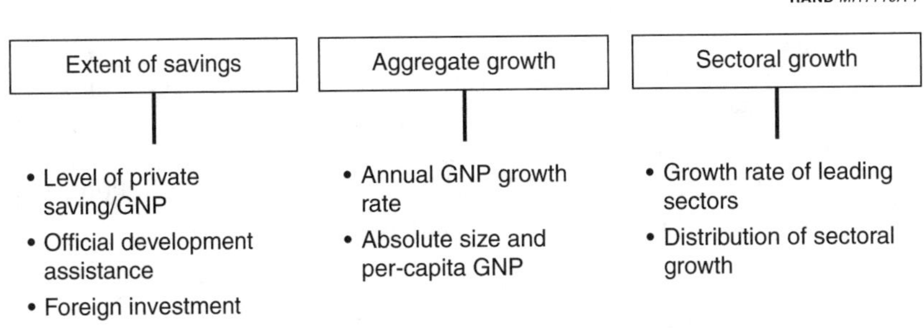

Figure 7—Capital and Illustrative Indicators

and more investment requires either greater domestic savings or foreign assistance. Domestic savings, carried out by individuals, households, firms, or government, can be generated either voluntarily through a reduction in consumption or involuntarily through taxation by, or compulsory lending to, the government. The absorption of underemployed labor into more productive work also constitutes a form of saving, though this is difficult to measure by standard indices. Savings from external sources can be garnered in the form of foreign direct assistance and direct and portfolio investments, the restriction of a country's imports (provided these are not substituted by increased domestic consumption), or an improvement in the terms of trade (assuming, of course, that the increased revenues are saved and not consumed). Measuring the sources of capital formation as a means of understanding a country's ability to provide usable investment resources must, therefore, focus on just the variables identified above. This includes measuring the overall rates of saving in the economy (disaggregated by source if needed), the ratio of taxes to GNP, and the economy's access to external resources in terms of official direct assistance, and foreign direct and portfolio investments.

When capital is accumulated through some combination of means such as those described above, the processes of growth produce a chain reaction that can be sustained only to the degree that a fraction of the growing incomes—generated either by increasingly roundabout consumption, greater economic widening, or faster technical change—is itself saved and plowed back into profitable enterprises so as to sustain the cycle indefinitely. Because this cycle occurs at different rates in different countries—given the wide disparity, inter alia, in levels of knowledge, rates of saving, and the character of technical change—the processes of capital accumulation produce different effects when measured by both the size and the growth rates of countries. Both these variables are important and need to be assessed when considering national power.

The size of a country in terms of its economic output is critical because output, in the first instance, represents a mass of resources that can be utilized for various purposes by a nation's political authority. Because national power is always relative, however, the size of a country's gross national product functions as a useful yardstick for how its capital stocks stand up to those of its competitors; a country with larger capital resources is not only afforded greater autonomy to choose its own preferred course of action but, ceteris paribus, also secures a greater measure of protection insofar as it can presumably produce larger and more effective military forces while simultaneously resolving the difficult tradeoffs involved in the production of such capabilities with greater flexibility than its less well-endowed neighbors. The size of an economy also brings other less well-recognized but equally critical benefits: because concentrations of economic power imply a concentration of capital resources, the wealthiest countries in effect possess the most "votes" in the global market economy. As a result, the global structure of production, the use and transfers of productive factors, and the exchange of raw materials, semifinished and finished goods, all comport with the pattern of preferences displayed by the largest group of consumers in the global economy, namely those economies with the largest capital resources or GNP. Larger economic size, therefore, not only bequeaths greater freedom of action but also structures the pattern of investment decisions in the global economy to its own advantage; it defines the nature and the extent of the bargains that can be struck in the international arena; and it affects the patterns of global access to resources because of the disproportionate weight of its own domestic consumers and investors.[42]

---

[42]Susan Strange, "What Is Economic Power and Who Has It?" *International Journal*, Vol. 30 (1975), pp. 207–224.

While size of capital resources in a gross sense is thus an important index of power, it must be refined in two ways. First, it is important to assess how the value of accumulated outputs or capital stacks up in the face of the size of the existing population. The measure of per-capita GNP thus becomes important because it describes a country's level of internal development in notional terms, while simultaneously providing some sense of the balance between internal and external demands on the country's resources. Per-capita GNP describes the size of the capital stocks per individual and thereby depicts the relative access to wealth and consumption within a country. It could therefore serve as a corrective measure in some cases insofar as it relates a stock measure of wealth to the number of people who must be supported by it.

Second, it is important to assess what proportion of a country's output derives from certain activities that are particularly important in the knowledge-based postindustrial age. Both GNP and per-capita GNP describe the levels of capital resources in aggregate and distributed terms respectively. They do not identify, however, how these capital resources are produced. In an age where the levels of actionable knowledge have become the yardstick by which power in general and effective coercive power in particular is produced, understanding whether a country's overall growth derives from certain leading-edge sectors as supposed to "sunset" sectors is important for assessing its power capabilities. As William R. Thompson points out, the link between relative power and dominance in the "leading sectors" of the global economy is critical.[43] The leading sectors in any given age are created by radical technological breakthroughs achieved in certain countries, and these sectors are crucial because in their early developmental stages, their positive impact on a country's economic growth is disproportionate to their size in relation to the overall economy. Moreover, dominance in the leading sectors is important to a country's ability to contend for geopolitical leadership in the international system. Thompson describes this link thus:

---

[43]William R. Thompson, "Long Waves, Technological Innovation, and Relative Decline," *International Organization*, Vol. 44 (Spring 1990), pp. 201–233.

> Major technological innovations are not only discontinuous in time and space, but the lead in innovational development . . . tends to be confined to a single national economy. This lead helps establish a commanding position in the pace of commercial, industrial, and economic growth. It also facilitates the development of the lead economy's commercial and financial centrality to the system. The movement toward increasingly productive commercial and financial centrality encourages the development of two other essential ingredients: the gradual ascendancy of a globally oriented, domestic ruling coalition and the creation of a politico-military infrastructure of global reach capabilities.[44]

Because the leading sectors today remain information and communications, understanding where the sources of accumulation lie in these areas provides a qualitative profile of the structure of capital generation in a country. Unfortunately, the standard division of the economy into the primary, secondary, and tertiary sectors hides more than it reveals in the postindustrial age. In large part, this is because the customary distinction between manufacturing and services is increasingly breaking down on one hand, while on the other hand the value of even traditional tangible goods is increasingly being lifted by the embedding of knowledge-based artifacts.[45] Thus, while it is useful to know the things national leaders traditionally worried about, like the share of manufacturing in both the GNP and the global product, today their ability to both know these things and assess their significance has dropped dramatically.[46] One solution to this problem might be to decompose the tertiary sector further into quaternary and quinary sectors, as Daniel Bell attempted in 1973.[47] Or it might be more useful to simply try to understand the extent of capital accumulation occurring in the knowledge-producing sectors of the economy as a means of appreciating the character of a country's GNP. There have been several efforts made at concep-

---

[44]Ibid., p. 224. As Thompson notes, historically, victory in global (or hegemonic) war has also been a stimulus to leading sector dominance and its concomitant effects.

[45]Danny Quah, *The Invisible Hand and the Weightless Economy,* Occasional Paper No. 12 (London: LSE Center for Economic Performance, 1996).

[46]Charles Goldfinger, "The Intangible Economy and Its Implications for Statistics and Statisticians," paper presented at the Eurostat-ISTAT seminar, Bologna, February 1996.

[47]Bell, op. cit., p. 117ff.

tualizing the structure of the knowledge-producing sectors of the economy: these include Bell at one end with three simple categories, Machlup and the OECD in the middle with five different categories each, and Porat and Rubin with eight expansive categories at the far end.[48] Some of these measures are better than others, but data organized on the basis of any of them would provide a useful comparative picture of how much of the GNP is owed to the knowledge-producing sectors of the economy.

Finally, the last measure of capital as a building block of national power must focus simply on the growth rate of GNP. This simple measure is important because it conveys information about the future size of the national economy (with all the benefits accruing to size), the changes in the balances of international power, and the ease with which a given country may be able to either increase its stock of coercive capabilities or change its factor endowments to garner the relatively greater increasing returns that may be accruing to certain critical sectors within the economy. Whether a country embarks on the latter choice, however, will be determined by its perception of the strategic value of certain sectors; the incremental capital-output ratio existing in that sector relative to others; and the rates of return accruing to investments in that sector in comparison to all other alternatives. In any event, GNP growth rates are important because they determine the choices that a country has with respect to developing its future national power.

On balance then, the value of capital, understood as a fund that represents a stock of capital goods possessed by a country, derives ultimately from its ability to make national sustained economic growth possible. To be sure, capital does not function as a "simple input" which when injected in "direct" form automatically produces increased productivity and rapid growth. Rather, its effectiveness derives in large measure from being a mediated input that often takes the form of better technical knowledge, improved human capital, more sophisticated machinery, and modernized forms of organi-

---

[48]Bell, op. cit.; Fritz Machlup, *The Production and Distribution of Knowledge in the United States* (Princeton: Princeton University Press, 1972); OECD, *Information Activities, Electronics and Telecommunication Technologies* (Paris: OECD, 1981); and M. Porat and M. Rubin, *The Information Economy: Development and Measurement* (Washington, D.C.: U.S. Government Printing Office, 1977).

zation in addition to its customary "raw" manifestation as money capital. Its contributions to increasing the stock of technical knowledge are particularly important from the viewpoint of national power, and in the postindustrial age this value will be increasingly manifested by the infrastructure that generates scientific and technological innovations within a given society.

PHYSICAL RESOURCES

The transformation of society from the agricultural age to the industrial age and beyond set into motion a process of economic change that resulted in new demands for various physical resources. Raw physical resources, in the form of land and national resources, had their greatest utility in the agricultural age. During the industrial age, energy sources acquired pride of place. In the postindustrial age, when knowledge-driven economic growth has become central to progress, the value of natural resources as a stock concept (with the exception of energy) appears to have decreased even further as technical knowledge provides new ways of utilizing existing natural resources more efficiently and, occasionally, even provides synthetic substitutes for depletable natural resources.

While the growth of knowledge has thus contributed to diminishing the importance of natural resources as inputs for economic growth, the rise of the international trading system has further reduced their relative significance. The existence of a fairly well institutionalized international trading system for primary commodities implies that countries need no longer be limited by the poverty of their natural endowments as far as their growth prospects and national power are concerned. This is all the more true because the number of absolutely critical raw materials has diminished over time, and even fewer of these materials are restricted in terms of single sources of supply. This is true today even for high-priority natural resources like energy.

Indicators of Physical Resources

Since natural resources in general are already lower-valued items in comparison to technology and human capital, it is unlikely that constraints with respect to both access and national endowments

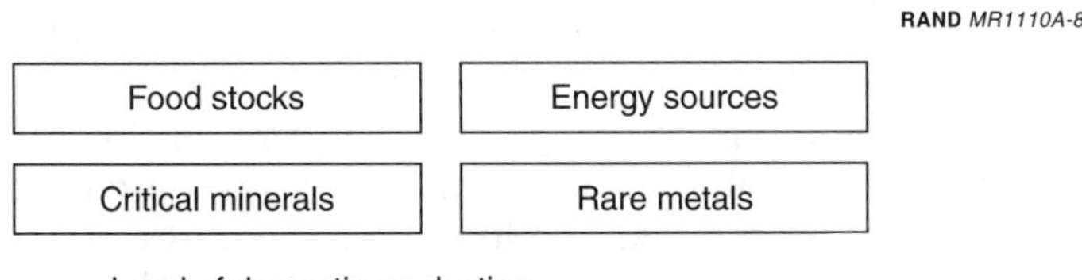

Figure 8—Physical Resources and Illustrative Indicators

would serve any more as real *impediments* to a nation's growth in power *so long as the international market for trade in primary commodities continues to function with reasonable efficiency.* This, at any rate, is likely to be true at least as far as most candidate great powers of interest to the United States are concerned.

The only exceptions to this rule may be energy and food (and, over the very long term, water), and the significance of these resources is as much technical as it is political: because energy and food remain inputs necessary for the functioning of about everything else in a modern economy, countries in general are extremely sensitive to the potential for disruption and cut-off in supply. Consequently, fossil fuel resources like oil, coal, and natural gas will continue to remain important, as will artificial fuel resources like nuclear power.

Peculiar to the postindustrial age, however, will be nonfuel resources like jewel bearings used in sophisticated machine tools and beryllium used with copper in electrical and computer components. Light, but strong and flexible metals like titanium, vanadium, chromium, cobalt, aluminum, and columbium, the vital components of complex machines, especially in the aerospace industry, will also remain significant. A set of other similar resources have also become critical with the progression of the information revolution. For instance, platinum group metals (iridium, palladium, and platinum) are critical components of information age electronics like circuit boards and computer network connectors; platinum is also used in the production of optical fibers for telecommunications. Germanium, a by-product of zinc processing, has become important for its use in high-data-rate optical communication systems, lasers, night-vision systems, and weapons guidance.[49] The aluminum by-product gallium arsenide has also received heightened attention because of its role as a component of high-speed integrated circuitry, especially relied upon in military computing. Silicon is another element that has received heightened attention because of the information age. Widely abundant, as the backbone of computer chips and fiber optics, silicon should not be ignored as a necessary building material. Lastly, the inputs for sophisticated materials technologies round out the list of critical information technologies. These inputs include the components of composite materials (graphite, carbon, asbestos, and other fibrous materials), and of ceramics (rare earth elements; pure, inorganic, nonmetallic powders; and fibers for reinforcement). These materials are increasingly vital to the production of sophisticated machinery (again, especially aerospace and weaponry). In addition, they have sparked interest in the possibility that synthetic materials might replace many former mineral dependencies.

When considering these resources as inputs of power, however, it is important to go beyond stockpiles and supplies to consider the accessibility of these resources during times of crisis, when states must rely largely on their own inputs for power. To measure this accessibility, both the obvious domestic sources and the degree to which these resources originate from stable external sources, i.e., allies or neutrals with stable governments, ought to be considered. This provides an indicator of the extent to which countries are dependent on vulnerable sources for the basic physical building blocks of power.

---

[49]Kenneth A. Kessel, *Strategic Minerals: U.S. Alternatives* (Washington, D.C.: National Defense University Press, 1990).

Chapter Six

MEASURING NATIONAL PERFORMANCE

The discussion about inputs for state power clearly underscores the fact that few—if any—such elements exist in raw "natural" form. Rather, these inputs are actually "intermediate goods," that is to say, resources created by prior societal or state actions with an eye to being incorporated in the production of still other "final goods." While the nature of the final goods is invariant in the realm of international politics—effective military instruments—the paths to their production may vary depending on the state-society structures of the country that produces them. A country with a strong society–weak state structure might seek to produce these intermediate goods mainly in order to produce commercial goods demanded by its civil society. A country with a strong state–weak society structure, in contrast, might concentrate on these intermediate goods simply in order to maximize the production of military instruments that enhance its national power in the international arena. Since the framework for measuring national power adopted here does not privilege one pattern of state-society relations or another, it does not matter *how* effective military capability is produced. It could be produced either indirectly, as a by-product of commercial endeavors (as in the case of countries with a strong society–weak state structure), or it could be produced directly (as in the case of countries with a strong state–weak society structure). Because effective military capability can be produced so long as a *minimally effective state or a minimally effective state-society complex exists*, the analytical task now consists of describing what exactly the predicates of these terms actually are.

This section of the framework, therefore, focuses on identifying and analyzing the mechanisms that enable countries to first produce the required inputs discussed above and then to convert these inputs into tangible, usable, national power in the form of effective military forces. As illustrated in Figure 9, it seeks to describe both those elements which *motivate* a country to produce the intermediate and final goods identified above and those variables which depict the levels of *state and societal performance* necessary if these intermediate and final goods are to be produced efficiently.

A country's ability to effectively produce these goods in the postindustrial age is seen to invariably derive from three factors: (1) the external constraints emerging from the international system; (2) the infrastructural capacity of its governing structures, "the state"; and (3) the ideational resources embedded in its state-society complex. Each of these variables will be analyzed in turn.

EXTERNAL CONSTRAINTS

All countries—nominally—have a choice about whether to acquire effective military capabilities. In practice, however, a country's freedom to choose is constrained by many factors, especially "structural" ones which refer to a country's spatial and hierarchic location in the international system. As Karen Rasler and William R. Thompson put it, "Political actors are free to make choices, but their choices are

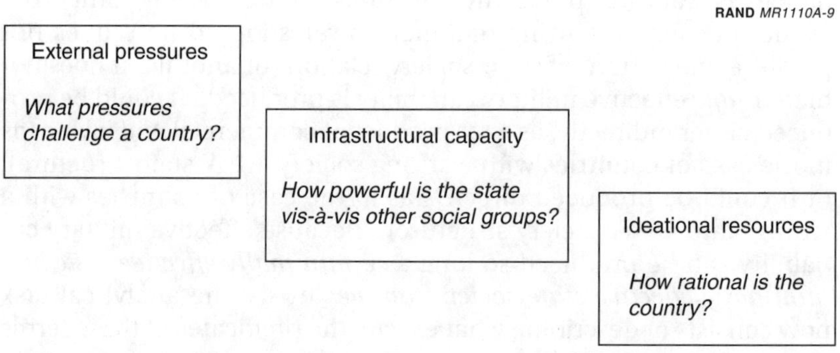

Figure 9—Factors Affecting National Performance

shaped by the structures and history they and their predecessors have made."[1] The historical record of international politics suggests that countries that fail to acquire effective military capabilities are threatened by a loss of security and autonomy, so not surprisingly, state managers invariably concentrate on developing the most effective military instruments possible either by exploiting the resources of their civil society or by producing these resources directly. The fate that befell 19th century China provides a good illustration of what can happen if a state ignores structural constraints.

The pressures on survival that emanate from the international system are thus the starting point for understanding how external pressures constrain countries to acquire effective military capabilities. The international system is no doubt a complex and multifaceted environment best described as a self-help system in which countries are concerned first and foremost with their survival.[2] In addition to self-help, however, the system has other disconcerting characteristics. It is characterized by: impure anarchy, which implies that entities vary in size and effective capabilities; the uncertainty of intentions, which implies that countries are never quite sure of the true objectives pursued by their competitors; the presence of varying growth rates, which implies that today's pygmies may become tomorrow's giants and vice versa; and uncertainty about the possibility, effectiveness, and durability of alliances, which implies that today's friends either may not remain friends or may not be very effective in providing for a common defense. In such an environment, where there is uncertainty about the level of effective protection available over time as well as about the future capabilities of other competitors, countries will experience varying degrees of insecurity as a result of the constantly shifting power relationships in the international system.[3]

---

[1]Karen Rasler and William R. Thompson, *War and State Making: The Shaping of the Global Powers* (Boston: Unwin and Hyman, 1989), p. 57.

[2]Waltz, *Theory of International Politics*, pp. 107, 127.

[3]This argument relating to the logic of domination, and those in the following six paragraphs, is amplified in Ashley J. Tellis, *The Drive to Domination: Towards a Pure Realist Theory of Politics*, unpublished Ph.D dissertation, The University of Chicago, 1994.

Each country will, therefore, seek to reduce this insecurity to the maximum degree possible—either through external balancing or internal growth or both—and this implies that it will attempt to increase its military capability to the maximum extent *over and above that possessed by others.* But because the military capabilities of countries constantly change, thanks to shifts in internal growth rates and/or balancing alignments, the struggle to reduce insecurity inevitably translates into a restless drive to continually strengthen one's own power capabilities while simultaneously enervating those of others. This dynamic persists because a country can be completely safe only when it is superior and not equal to or weaker than its competitors. As a result, while external balancing may appear as the necessary behavior of weaker countries designed to ensure security in the first instance, maintaining *balances* cannot be the structure-engendered imperative *sufficient* to ensure durable national security in perpetuity.

This conclusion may be further elaborated in the following way: In a competitive environment, where security is finite and where safety is a function of possessing a differential advantage in relative military power, a strategy of ensuring balances alone—that is, being merely strong enough to equalize another entity's power—cannot suffice. Such equalization of power inevitably provokes mutual anticipatory violence; it puts a premium on quickly developing strategies that produce victory even in the absence of superior numbers; and it inevitably results in the unavoidable elimination of some competitors in the short run. Since no country prefers to be such an eliminated competitor, it is obvious that none will be content with equalizing balances to begin with. Even if the phenomenon of mutual anticipatory violence (together with its disastrous consequences for some) is momentarily overlooked, it is evident that equalizing power as a strategy of guaranteeing survival is just as, if not more, problematic over the long run. This is because a country can never be certain that the present capacity to harm possessed by its competitors will not increase over time, thanks to either internal growth, external alignments, or external conquests. If such potential increases in coercive capacity do in fact accrue to another country diachronically, it would create a situation where both the scarce resources available systemwide and the military protection possessed by a particular country will decrease at some foreseeable point in the future. Given this possibility, no country can be fully reassured simply by the possession of equalizing military capabilities today.

More important, however, no country can be fully reassured even if it has military capabilities superior to those of its competitors, because in a situation defined by uneven international growth (whether accruing from internal development, external alignments, or external conquests) and uncertainty about where and when such growth takes place, countries would fear that their present superiority and, by implication, their future security could be at risk at some eventual point in time. As a result, both equalizing another's power *and* being *presently* superior to another does not guarantee the future security that all countries, which are "global"[4] maximizers, necessarily seek.

This global maximization of security can be ensured only if a country can be stronger than other countries all the time, or in other words, only when a country enjoys permanent superiority over others. Even though such permanent superiority may be unattainable, given that uneven international growth is the norm in international politics, the structure of security competition nonetheless condemns every country to attempt seeking it. This quest for permanent superiority acquires particular saliency because seeking anything less may entail elimination—an unacceptable alternative because every rational egoist, both isolated individuals and organized entities like countries, fears above all, in Hobbes' words, that "terrible enemy of nature, death, from which [it] expect[s] both the loss of all power, and also the greatest of all bodily pains in the losing."[5] Given the unpalatable choice between the worst outcome of elimination and the lesser but still highly repellent outcome of subjugation (or the loss of autonomy), it is no surprise to find that each country—in an effort to avoid both choices—continually strives to increase the margins of available power relative to others. That is, each country tries to maximize its own protective capabilities at the expense of others at every moment in time either by eliminating or subjugating or subordinating as many of its competitors as it presently can, all while continuously

[4]The notion of "global" maximization essentially refers to the desire of agents to maximize certain values not across space but across time. "Global" maximization, thus, refers to intertemporal maximization in contrast to "local" maximization, which is oriented to maximizing certain values at a given point in time.

[5]Thomas Hobbes, *The Elements of Law* (Bristol: Thoemmes Press, 1994) ,p. 54.

attempting to increase its internal growth to the maximum possible level. Every country—whether strong or weak—therefore seeks to dominate the international system where and while (and to the extent) it can, simply in order to preemptively forestall the possibility of being decisively disadvantaged with respect to security during some future period. The structure constrains this behavior; what simply differs is how it is carried out. The strong, because they can, strive to dominate alone. The weak, because they must, attempt to either ward off domination by others or seek to dominate themselves through transitory mutual collaboration.

The logical necessity of striving to dominate thus derives essentially from the fact that domination promises a greater degree of protection and autonomy when shifts in protective and coercive capabilities are constantly occurring throughout the international system at uneven and unpredictable rates. Nicholas Spykman, for example, captured this insight succinctly in the following terms:

> The truth of the matter is that states are interested only in a balance which is in their favor. Not an equilibrium, but a generous margin is their objective. There is no real security in being just as strong as a potential enemy; there is security only in being a little stronger. There is no possibility of action if one's strength is fully checked; there is a chance for a positive foreign policy only if there is a margin of force which can be freely used. Whatever the theory and rationalization, the practical objective is the constant improvement of the state's own relative power position. The balance desired is the one which neutralizes other states, leaving the home state free to be the deciding force and the deciding voice.[6]

Similarly, Robert Gilpin, corroborating this argument further, notes that structural necessity "stimulates, and may compel, a state to increase its power; at the least, it necessitates that the prudent state prevent relative increases in the power of competitor states."[7]

This conclusion, it must be admitted, is derived primarily from a pure theory of conflict where countries, being treated essentially as

---

[6]Nicholas Spykman, *America's Strategy in World Politics* (New York: Harcourt, Brace, 1942), pp. 21–22.

[7]See Gilpin, *War and Change in World Politics*, pp. 87–88.

"billiard balls" without any historical or locational attributes, are seen to be in incessant competition with one another. In the real world of international politics, however, the vast majority of countries are usually not actively involved in the contentious struggle for order-production witnessed at the core of the international system. While these countries certainly struggle to dominate their local environments in order to continually assure security over time, these struggles go unnoticed for the most part, since they do not affect either the course or the defining outcomes in international politics. These latter developments are conditioned primarily by the actions of the great and the near-great powers, and these entities no doubt deserve the most attention in any analysis of national power, in part because all potential challengers to the United States for global hegemony would come from within these two categories. The conclusion about the universal propensity of all countries to dominate, however, serves as a cautionary reminder against any easy assertion of "strategic exceptionalism" in international politics: while most national actions will never be significant from the perspective of the global system, these actions could indeed have very consequential results if one or more of the currently less well-endowed countries were to dramatically increase their national capabilities at some point in the future.

It is important to recognize, therefore, that the universal structure-constrained dynamic of attempting to dominate brings in its wake two important effects.

First, it results in a pattern of isomorphic behavior, that is, countries are forced to behave similarly with respect to the challenges they face in the production of adequate security. This similarity of response is a product of the pervasive constancy of the constraining structure, and it represents a specific manifestation of the isomorphic pattern identified by organizational theory. Isomorphism explains why organizations, although they perform a myriad of different functions, tend to be alike in form and practice. As Paul Di Maggio and Walter Powell observe, "the theory of isomorphism addresses not the psychological states of actors but the structural determinates of the range of choices that actors perceive as rational or prudent."[8] Isomorphic behaviors are especially likely to occur in realms that are highly structured, where individual entities are subjected to the same environmental conditions.[9] Thus, it is not surprising that a similarity of responses from their constituent units is often seen in competitive realms such as the market and in the international political system.[10] But these similar responses, it must be noted, have two distinct but related dimensions: "What" is to be done, meaning the kind of response appropriate to the situation, is regulated entirely by the rational calculating nature of the entities that populate the international system. Since every action, however, has both logical and empirical components, individual countries may often need knowledge of others' successful performance if they are to increase their power adequately. "How" things are to be done, therefore, may be learned or imitated, especially in an environment where information about the "choice of techniques" is either costly to acquire or is imperfectly distributed. Some facets of similar national behaviors (especially those relating to knowledge-related issues connected with the choice of techniques) may, therefore, be attributed to "learning" in international politics. But such "learning" is less an example of "socialization," at least understood as "some kind of training through which . . . [an entity] . . . is led to internalize norms, values, attitudes, roles, knowledge of facts, and know-how that will make up a kind of syllabus designed to be achieved later on, more or less mechanically,"[11] than it is a manifestation of "optimization," where the "observed uniformity among [entitative behaviors], derive[s] from an

---

[8]Paul J. Di Maggio and Walter K. Powell, "The Iron Cage Revisited: Institutional Isomorphism and Collective Rationality in Organizational Fields," *American Political Science Review,* Vol. 48 (April 1983), p. 149, note 4.

[9]Amos Hawley, "Human Ecology," in D. Sills (ed.), *International Encyclopedia of the Social Sciences* (Princeton: Princeton University Press, 1968), p. 334. Also see Howard E. Aldrich, *Organizations and Environments* (Englewood Cliffs, NJ: Prentice-Hall, 1979).

[9]Ibid., p. 219.

[10]As Hannan and Freeman observe, "Isomorphism can arise from purposeful adaptation of organizations to the common constraints they face or because nonisomorphic organizations are selected against." Michael T. Hannan and John Freeman, "The Population Ecology of Organizations," *American Journal of Sociology,* Vol. 82, No. 5 (1977), pp. 929–964.

[11]Boudon and Bourricaud, op. cit., p. 357.

evolutionary, adopting, competitive system employing a criterion of survival, which can operate independently of individual motivations."[12]

Second, the drive to dominate forces countries to restructure their domestic political arrangements and their state-societal investment patterns and allocation decisions to maximize the production of those intermediate and final goods necessary for the production of adequate national power. This effect is highlighted powerfully by the "second image reversed" perspective in international relations theory, which posits a linkage between the international system's structural constraints and a state's domestic structure. Charles Tilly's famous aphorism, "War made the state, and the state made war" neatly captures the concept.[13] In his historical work, Tilly has showed how the need to protect against external danger compelled countries in early modern Europe to develop administrative and bureaucratic structures to maintain, supply, and finance permanent military establishments. But there is more to it than that: other historical case studies have suggested how the creation of effective military power, especially that connected to great power emergence, actually reflects a country's *internal* adjustment to the international system's structural constraints.[14] The German historian Otto Hintze elaborated on this point by observing that the way in which countries are organized internally often reflects "their position relative to each other and their overall position in the world" and that "throughout the ages pressure from without has been a determining influence on [the] internal structure" of countries."[15] Hintze's discussion of

---

[12]Armen A. Alchian, "Uncertainty, Evolution, and Economic Theory," *Journal of Political Economy,* Vol. 58, No. 3 (June 1950), p. 219.

[13]Charles Tilly, "Reflections on the History of European State Making," in Charles Tilly (ed.), *The Formation of National States in Western Europe* (Princeton: Princeton University Press, 1975), p. 42.

[14]See Christopher Layne, "The Unipolar Illusion: Why New Great Powers Will Rise," *International Security,* Vol. 17, No. 4 (Spring 1993), pp. 5–55.

[15]Otto Hintze, "Military Organization and the Organization of the State," in Felix Gilbert (ed.), *The Historical Essays of Otto Hintze* (Princeton: Princeton University Press, 1975), p. 183. Also see the discussion of Hintze's views in Felix Gilbert, "From Clausewitz to Delbruck and Hintze," *Journal of Strategic Studies,* Vol. 3 (1980), pp. 11–20.

Prussia-Germany and England is illustrative.[16] The domestic, political, and economic systems of both these countries developed dissimilarly, in large part because each was affected differently by international pressures. Maritime England, for example, was far more secure relative to continental Germany. But, as is true otherwise, Prussia-Germany and England were very much alike in other crucial respects. That is, both countries organized their state apparatus for war and trade in order to maximize their security in a competitive international environment.

The structural pressures emanating from the international system, therefore, function as the primary motivating influence that causes countries to increase their national power. By forcing countries to attempt domination merely in order to preserve themselves over time, the structure of international politics constrains them to become more sensitive to the character of their resource endowments and military capabilities as well as to the nature of their internal state structures. But because the international system is not composed of equal-sized countries, the intensity of systemic pressures will not be felt evenly among its constituent parts. The larger countries, the more important countries, and the strategically located countries will feel the pressures of structural necessity more than others in large part because they have greater assets to protect or because they possess certain resources that others covet. For these reasons, these countries will devote relatively disproportionate attention to their national power even though the pressure to dominate as a prudent method of ensuring national survival affects all countries in the international system.

The challenge therefore now consists of being able to translate this notion of external pressure into components that are measurable at least in an estimative, if not in a quantitative, sense. Taking cues from the discussion above, these pressures, illustrated in Figure 10, can be assessed along three broad dimensions: the nature of the external threat facing the country, the nature of its state interests, and the nature of its political aims.

---

[16]Hintze, "Military Organization and the Organization of the State."

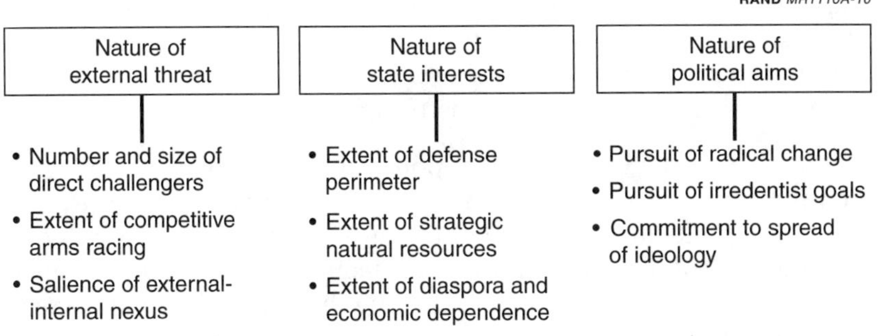

Figure 10—Analyzing External Constraints

Since fear is a powerful incentive for countries to increase their national power, countries that are threatened by others—or perceive that they are threatened—are likely to be highly motivated to increase their resources and their military capabilities necessary to enhance national survival. The extent of this motivating fear deriving from external threats can be judged by assessing (i) the number and relative size of the direct challengers or rivals facing the country; (ii) the extent of external support for any internal challenges facing the country; (iii) the extent of any direct sources of friction, like territorial disputes or ideological conflicts; and (iv), the extent of any competitive arms-racing that the country in question may participate in.

Since countries with expanding interests also have strong incentives to acquire or increase their national power, discerning a country's interests would also provide a way to assess the motivating effects of external pressures. The nature and extent of a country's interest could be judged along the following lines: (i) its geographic location and the extent of its defensive perimeter, with location identifying its geopolitical value and its defensive perimeter indicating both the areas it must actively defend and those it has an interest in; (ii) the extent of its strategic natural resources (and possibly its composition of trade), these variables indicating whether it has resources that may be coveted by others as well as the extent of its external dependency; (iii) the extent of and commitment to its natural diaspora, indicating the extent of the critical political commitments it may have to service *in extremis*; and (iv) the relative rate of growth of its projectible military power and its economic strength, with the former variable indicating the increased risk of conflict with others and the latter suggesting the growing stakes and interests in the international distribution of power, prestige, and wealth which will eventually be defended by means of military instruments.

Since countries with revisionist political aims also have strong incentives to increase their national power, assessing the nature of a country's political aims also contributes to providing a more complete picture of the external pressures facing a state. Here it is useful to discern whether a country is pursuing the goal of (i) securing radical changes of the established international order through force, or (ii) recovering irredentist claims, or (iii) promoting ideological proselytization. If a country appears to be preparing to use force to alter the geopolitical status quo for any of these reasons, it will in all likelihood not only want to increase its national power but actually want to ensure that its military forces are "ready to go" and have the capabilities to prevail over its likely opponents.[17]

INFRASTRUCTURAL CAPACITY

War and "state building" are inextricably linked phenomena. The presence of external threat has always been a potent factor driving the consolidation of countries, the rise of great powers, and the internal expansion of state power. External pressures are important because they affect a state's *incentives* to develop the political capacity to extract and mobilize assets from its society to support its external policies. It is no surprise, therefore, that research generally indicates that the greater the external pressures, the more highly mobilized a state is likely to be. The more highly a state mobilizes, the greater its ability to penetrate society and to extract wealth from the country at large.[18]

---

[17]Barry Posen, *The Sources of Military Doctrine: France, Britain, and Germany Between the World Wars* (Ithaca: Cornell University Press, 1984), p. 74.

[18]For example, see Tilly, *The Formation of National States in Europe,* op. cit.; Karen Rasler and William R. Thompson, *War and State Making: The Shaping of the Global Powers* (Boston: Unwin and Hyman, 1989); A.F.K. Organski and Jacek Kugler, *The War Ledger* (Chicago: University of Chicago Press, 1980); Richard Bean, "War and the Birth of the Nation State," *Journal of Economic History,* Vol. 33 (1977), pp. 203–221; Keith Jaggers, "War and the Three Faces of Power: War Making and State Making in Europe and America," *Comparative Political Studies,* Vol. 25, No. 1 (April 1992), pp. 26–62; and

The impact of external constraints, however, is only half the story. The state still must frame and implement *internal* policies that will invest it with the political capacity to extract wealth from society. Whether the state in fact is able to acquire this political capacity depends, in large part, on the role of national leadership and institutions.[19] Indeed, as Paul Y. Hammond observed, the question of how much the state should extract from its internal political and economic system to pursue its external goals is both crucial and fundamental.[20] The answer to this question is shaped not merely by the availability of physical resources. Indeed, for most countries, physical resource availability, per se, is seldom a limiting factor. This is especially true in the postindustrial age, when the value of physical resources relative to other inputs has dropped considerably. More important than the availability of physical assets, therefore, is the state's political capacity to extract wealth from its society in order to *develop* the comprehensive resource base necessary for a productive economic system.[21] The inability of some states to both adequately extract wealth from their societies and transform that wealth into intermediate goods that can be used to produce effective military instruments gives rise to "the paradox of unrealized power."[22] The *political performance of the state*, therefore, functions as the crucial link between potential and effective power, and the discussion in this section focuses entirely on understanding how the political performance of the state ought to be conceptualized and measured.

In discussing issues relating to state performance, it is important to reiterate and amplify the distinction between "country" and "state" drawn earlier. The former term, it must be understood, is essentially iconic and describes an aggregated entity that has spatial dimen-

---

Aristide Zolberg, "Strategic Interactions and the Formation of Modern States: France and England," *International Social Science Journal*, Vol. 32, No. 4 (1980), pp. 687–716.

[19]Jaggers, op. cit., p. 29.

[20]Paul Y. Hammond, "The Political Order and the Burden of External Relations," *World Politics*, Vol. 19 (1967), p. 443.

[21]See Alan C. Lamborn, "Power and the Politics of Extraction," *International Studies Quarterly*, Vol. 27 (1983), pp. 125–146; Lewis W. Snider, "Identifying the Elements of State Power: Where Do We Begin?" *Comparative Political Studies*, Vol. 20, No. 3 (October 1987), pp. 314–356.

[22]David A. Baldwin, "Power Analysis and World Politics: New Trends Versus Old Tendencies," *World Politics*, Vol. 31, No. 2 (January 1979), pp. 163–194.

sions, physical resources, population, and governing institutions. The latter term, in contrast, is narrower and, far from being iconic, actually encodes directive capacity since it refers specifically to the governing institutions that preside over the spatially extended entity otherwise labeled the "country." All discussions involving the term "state," therefore, refer expressly to the capability of governing institutions and must not be misconstrued as simply another nominalistic expression for "country."

While the distinction between "country" and "state" is therefore critical, there is little doubt that the latter term is itself "a messy concept,"[23] since it embodies several distinct, though related, elements: (1) differentiated institutions run by its own personnel; (2) central political control of a distinct political territory with political relations radiating outward from the seat of national authority to the rest of its domain; (3) a monopoly of authoritative, binding rule-making; and (4) a claimed monopoly on the legitimate use of coercive force.[24] These differentiated facets notwithstanding, the state ultimately can be understood as a territorially grounded "coercion-wielding organization" that seeks to defend its territory from external threat while simultaneously suppressing challenges to national authority that emanate from within.[25] In short, these twin tasks imply that "the state is the gatekeeper between intrasocietal and extrasocietal flows of action."[26]

Within the territory over which the state presides is society (sometimes called civil society). Society comprises both organiza-

---

[23]Michael Mann, "The Autonomous Power of the State," *Archives Europeenes de Sociologie,* Vol. 25, No. 2 (1984), p. 187. See also J. P. Nettl, "The State as a Conceptual Variable," *World Politics* (1968), pp. 559–592.

[24]Mann, "The Autonomous Power of the State," p. 188; John A. Hall and John Ikenberry, *The State* (Minneapolis: University of Minnesota Press, 1989), pp. 1–2; Joel Migdal, *Strong Societies and Weak States: State-Society Relations and State Capabilities in the Third World* (Princeton: Princeton University Press, 1988), pp. 18–19; Dietrich Rueschemeyer and Peter B. Evans, "The State and Economic Transformation," in Peter B. Evans, Dietrich Rueschemeyer, and Theda Skocpol (eds.), *Bringing the State Back In* (Cambridge: Cambridge University Press, 1985), pp. 46–47; and Charles Tilly, "On the History of European State-Making," in Charles Tilly (ed.), *The Formation of National States in Europe* (Princeton: Princeton University Press, 1975), p. 27.

[25]Tilly, *Coercion, Capital, and European States,* p. 1.

[26]Nettl, op. cit., p. 564.

tions and actors, for example: individuals, classes, ethnic and religious groups, villages, and "strongmen." In this environment, the state constantly seeks to acquire (or, if it has acquired, to maintain) the exclusive power to impose the "rules of the game" on society. As Joel Migdal observes:

> These game rules involve much more than broad constitutional principles; they include the written and unwritten laws, regulations, decrees, and the like, which state officials indicate they are willing to enforce through the coercive means at their disposal. [The] rules encompass everything from living up to contractual commitments to driving on the right side of the road to paying alimony on time. They involve the entire array of property rights and countless definitions of the boundaries of acceptable behavior for people.[27]

But if the state is weak, the social environment over which it presides will resist all its attempts at imposing the rules of the game. The state, in such circumstances, may be unable to impose the kind of social control that results in "the successful subordination of people's own inclinations of social behavior or behavior sought by other social organizations in favor of the behavior prescribed by national rules."[28]

If the state either cannot or will not impose social control of this sort, it will find itself locked in a struggle with other societal actors for rule-making primacy:

> These struggles are not over precisely which laws the state should enact or how the state's laws or constitution should be interpreted; these, after all, are decided within state organs, legislatures, and courts. Instead, these struggles are much more fundamental, reaching beyond marginal deviance and beyond the formal roles of any existing political institutions in the society. These struggles are over whether the state will be able to displace or harness other organizations—families, clans, multinational corporations, domestic enterprises, tribes, patron-client dyads—which make the rules against the wishes and goals of state leaders.[29]

---

[27]Migdal, *Strong Societies and Weak States*, p. 14.

[28]Ibid., p. 22.

[29]Ibid., p. 31.

States that are unable to attain effective social control at this fundamental level will have difficulty in extracting and mobilizing the resources needed to support the country's external policy, especially those policies mandated by the constraints of international politics which revolve around the imperative to dominate for purposes of assuring security. Indeed, as Mann notes, "a prime motivation for state leaders to attempt to stretch the state's rule-making domain within its formal boundaries, even with all the risks that has entailed, has been to build sufficient clout to survive the dangers posed by those outside its boundaries, from the world of states."[30] The interplay between the state and society is thus crucial for understanding whether a particular country will be able to mobilize its resources effectively and convert them into usable military power. As Kugler and Domke convincingly argue,

> The foundation of power in the global system is the relationship between state and society. Governments acquire the tools of political influence through the mobilization of human and material resources for national action. However, this linkage is usually overlooked in the literature of international politics, because power politics and the system structure perspective seldom deal with changes in domestic structures and their impact on the global system.[31]

So to assess whether the state is likely to be successful in extracting and mobilizing societal wealth in order to produce the resources necessary to create effective military power, one must be able to analyze the relative distribution of power between the state and society. Here, the standard distinction[32] between "strong" or "weak" states in relation to the degree of social control they exercise over society may be misleading on two counts. First, state capabilities in relation to society are dynamic, not static. This implies that "gaining, exercising and maintaining state capacity is an extremely complicated matter, in which there . . . [is] . . . a perpetual dialectic between the state

---

[30]Ibid., p. 21.

[31]Jacek Kugler and William Domke, "Comparing the Strength of Nations," *Comparative Political Studies*, Vol. 19, No. 1 (April 1986), p. 40.

[32]Katzenstein, op. cit. See also Stephen D. Krasner, *Defending the National Interest* (Princeton: Princeton University Press, 1978).

seizing and being granted authority."[33] State and societal capabilities vis-à-vis one another will wax and wane over time, and all analyses of state-society relationships must therefore be sensitive to the transitory character of the existing internal national balances of power. Second, often it is not sufficient to say that the state is strong in relationship to society, because state power is usually uneven across policy areas.[34] Because a state may be strong with respect to some functional areas but weak in some others, it is necessary to specify the functional areas in which the state is strong, or at the very least it is important to investigate whether the state is minimally effective in the key area of concern to this analysis: national security. Bearing these two considerations in mind, the following discussion will attempt to capture the nature of state-society relations in terms of the concept of "infrastructural" capacity.

The infrastructural power or capacity of a state may be summarized as deriving from the dynamics between state and society over issues of "self-motivation" or purpose. Infrastructural capacity is the power that enables a state to manage, cope with, or otherwise transform internal and external stress in support of its goals.[35] Consequently, infrastructural capacity is internal: it is the potential of a state to unilaterally motivate itself to develop its resources toward its goals, and Mann defines it as "the capacity of the state to actually penetrate civil society and to implement logistically political decisions throughout the realm."[36] The character and extent of a state's infrastructural power is critical for the production and transformation of resources that allow it to both dominate the cycles of economic innovation and develop the requisite hegemonic potential in the form of effective military capabilities such that a state with greater infrastructural capability will be better equipped to develop these foundations of national power in comparison to a state with

---

[33]Hall and Ikenberry, *The State*, p. 14.

[34]Theda Skocpol, "Bringing the State Back In: Strategies of Analysis in Current Research," in Evans, Rueschemeyer, and Skocpol (eds.), *Bringing the State Back In*, p. 17. As Krasner notes, "There is no reason to assume a priori that the pattern of strengths and weaknesses will be the same for all policies." Krasner, op. cit., p. 58.

[35]Mann, op. cit.

[36]Mann, op. cit., p. 189.

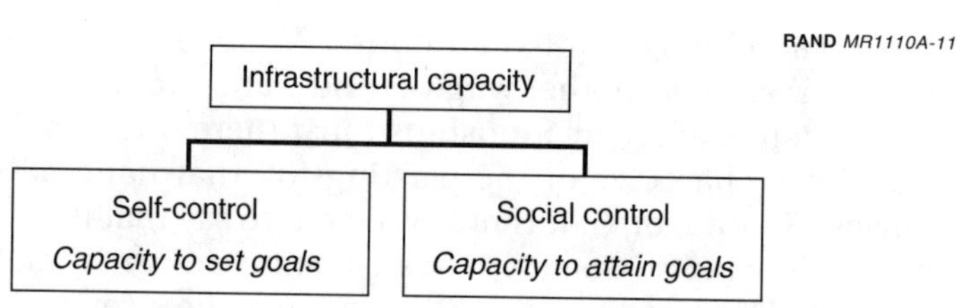

Figure 11—Understanding Infrastructural Capacity

less infrastructural capability.[37] *Greater infrastructural power thus translates into greater economic and military capability which, in turn, translates into greater national power.* As illustrated in Figure 11, a state's infrastructural capacity is manifested along two broad dimensions.

Self-Control

The first dimension of infrastructural capacity is the ability of the state to define its goals. This ability, which can be termed self-control, is often overlooked or assumed away since it is usually supposed that countries are rational, unitary actors with purposive goals that are both easily recognized and consistently pursued. Moreover, it is assumed all too easily that there is a consensus among state managers charged with the pursuit of these goals. In theory, therefore, countries are often simply assumed to have self-control.[38] What is assumed in theory, however, is often not evident in reality. In prac-

[37]It should be noted, however, that infrastructural power, an internal power to shape its destiny, is distinct from a state's power relative to other states. Such relative power also bears on the way a state develops resources, and this dynamic is addressed under the rubric of external constraints.

[38]Self-control, or the power to set goals, is not the same as the power that determines the content of the goals a state sets. This distinction is important because it suggests that effective state capacity requires at least two different kinds of capability: the ability to define goals, and the ability to define the content of those goals in a manner conducive to the predicates of power in the postindustrial age. The ability to define the content of the goals in a manner commensurate with the postindustrial age draws more on ideational resources than on infrastructural capacity, and will be discussed in a later section.

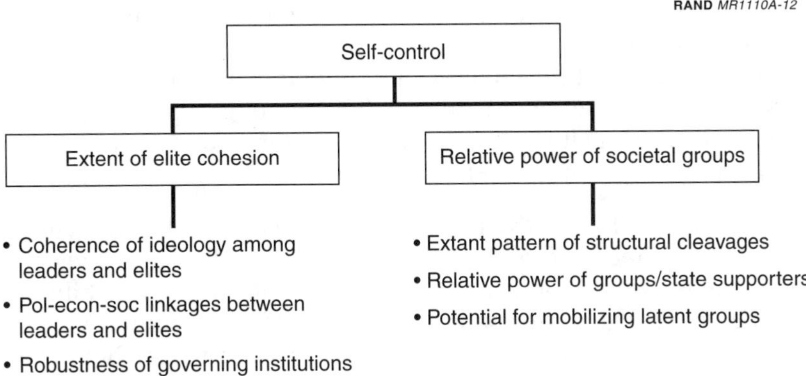

Figure 12—"Self-Control" and Illustrative Indicators

tice, the interactions between the two spheres of state and society are generally quite disorderly, and together they are not necessarily predisposed to controlled goal-setting. Further, the state itself generally consists of numerous, graded hierarchies rather than a single locus of decisionmaking and leadership. And while the boundaries of the state vis-à-vis society are obvious in theory, in practice these boundaries too are subject to the pressure of societal persuasion in the face of changes in state strength. Finally, societal pressure groups also have disparate, often contradictory, goals in themselves. The end result of all these factors is that the impulses contributing to the definition of national goals do not necessarily, or even frequently, converge. Given all of this, a state's ability to recognize and articulate goals for itself should not be taken for granted in any serious analysis of national power.

Extent of elite cohesion. The extent of a state's capacity for self-control therefore merits independent analysis, and this requires an understanding of the sources of that control. Since this variable refers to the ability to engage in effective goal-setting, it must almost by definition be rooted in the structures, framework, and processes of societal decisionmaking. More specifically, the societal decisionmaking context most relevant to the capacity for self-control is the public sphere of politics, since the very existence of a "national project," or a set of specific goals and objectives, presupposes the acquiescence, if not the approval, of the most powerful sector of society. This implies that the state's capacity for self-control is inexorably a function of the coherence exhibited by its political elite, an entity that can be defined as those individuals or groups who possess varying degrees of either high traditional status, economic influence, administrative power, or coercive capacity.

The existence of a consensus among state elites would indicate a greater likelihood of goal-setting success, while stark divisions among elites would indicate either unstable goals or an inability to pursue national goals normally associated with the accouterments of power. The existence of such a consensus, however, does not in any way imply the absence of personal or social competition among elites. Elite competition is a staple of political life and will exist in any society. So long as the competition is about access to power and not about fundamental national goals, a state may be said to possess the requisite measure of self-control. Even competition about national goals may be useful, if it is renewing as opposed to destructive. That is, competition about goals that takes place in an orderly fashion with the intent of bringing about a societal consensus for certain kinds of investments connected with producing national power is emblematic of self-control, in contrast to a competition that involves a struggle for increased rents by certain "distributional coalitions" that bear little relevance to the objective of enhancing national power. Therefore, so long as state managers have a fairly coherent view of what is required for national power or are at least willing to debate the requirements for national power through ordered political processes, the state in question may be deemed to exhibit self-control.

The relative cohesion of the governing elite, thus, remains the first dimension of a state's capacity to control its destiny, at least as far as effective goal-setting is concerned. Moreover, the more cohesive an elite is, the more committed it would be to the effective execution of its decisions. *Thus, greater elite cohesion results in greater self-control, which in turn results in an enhanced ability to set goals, which finally results in an increased capacity to augment national power.* How can the relative cohesion of the political elite be evaluated? In principle, this can be done in multiple ways, but all require qualitative judgments by analysts familiar with the domestic politics of a given country. Specific indicators here include the consistency of the ideology and rhetoric issuing from key elite actors to the public; the internal organizational and social linkages between the state managers and elite; the nature, durability, and effectiveness of higher political institutions; and the robustness of shared norms among key members of the regime and the social bases of their support.

Relative power of societal groups. While the extent of elite cohesion remains a key variable affecting the ability of states to set goals, the second dimension of self-control pertains to the relative power of various societal groups within a country. The nature of societal groupings within a country is critical to self-control because it speaks to the issue of national cohesion and, more specifically, the ability of state managers and their supporting elites to mobilize the masses in support of certain strategic policies aimed at enhancing national power. A lack of cohesion deriving from the existence of deep-seated social cleavages rooted either in class, religious, linguistic, ethnic, or regional fissures undermines the state's mobilization capabilities in three ways. First, internal fragmentation compromises the state's legitimacy. Unlike competition between political interest groups, which the state can resolve by carrot (economic inducements) and stick (coercion) tactics, ethnic, religious, and linguistic divisions in particular "tend to be diffuse and all-embracing rather than instrumental and therefore respond less readily to state policy."[39] Also, the existence of such cleavages undercuts the state's claim to represent the "universal particularism" of society's norms and interests.[40] Second, a lack of cohesion due to ethnic or religious cleavages can weaken the state's ability to project power externally by compelling it to divert resources from national security to internal security.[41] Third, the fissures that exist in society generally may be reflected in the state's military forces. This serves to reduce unit cohesion and

---

[39]Dietrich Rueschemeyer and Peter B. Evans, "The State and Economic Transformation: Toward an Analysis of the Conditions Underlying Effective Intervention," in Evans, Rueschemeyer, and Skocpol (eds.), op. cit., p. 65.

[40]Ibid.

[41]Stephen Peter Rosen, *Societies and Military Power: India and Its Armies* (Ithaca: Cornell University Press, 1996), pp. vii–ix. As Rosen observes, "In terms of offensive power, internal social divisions can increase the amount of military power needed to maintain internal domestic order, reducing the surplus of military power that can be projected abroad."

morale, and it produces an overall reduction in the effectiveness of the state's military forces.[42]

So while the ideal condition—from the perspective of effective self-control—is one where no serious social cleavages exist in a country, it is unrealistic to expect such a reality in the empirical world of politics. *All* countries have social cleavages of one sort or another, each with varying degrees of seriousness. When examining a state's capacity to effectively set goals, then, it is more important to focus on whether the cleavages in question actually impede the ability of state managers to make the requisite decisions associated with acquiring or increasing national power. Toward that end, it is important to examine three distinct sets of issues relating to the social structures of a given country. First, it is necessary to establish the extent and pattern of structural cleavages simply in order to paint a "social map" of the country's patterns of political, economic, and social interaction. Second, the strength of existing state managers must be discerned at two levels: (i) the extent of support state managers can garner from certain privileged elites in society, and (ii) the extent of power held by the state managers and their supporting elites vis-à-vis other mobilized social groups in society who may seek national goals different from those being currently pursued. Third, the existence of other latent groups, who may share affinities based on class, religious, linguistic, ethnic, or regional divisions, must be discerned. Their potential for mobilization must be assessed and the consequences of their mobilization for the future of the national goals associated with the pursuit of power must be analyzed.[43]

If, when the constellation and depth of intrastate divisions are thus assessed, it is found that the balance of power sufficiently favors state managers (and their supporting elites), it may be concluded that the state as an institution has the requisite self-control in that it is capable of setting certain goals and pursuing them effectively without any debilitating hindrance from other social competitors within the country. This, of course, presumes that there is sufficient coherence

---

[42]Ibid.

[43]For an extended discussion of mapping patterns of political closure, see Ashley J. Tellis, Thomas S. Szayna, and James Winnefield, *Anticipating Ethnic Conflict* (Santa Monica, CA: RAND, MR-853-A, 1997).

among state leaders and their social bases of support themselves, but if such exists, then a favorable social balance of power is all that is required for the possession of self-control understood as the capacity to effectively set certain goals and pursue them.

Social Control

The ability to make a decision or set a goal is not the same as the ability to take action on that decision or to actually fulfill the goal. Social control is the second kind of power in the domain of infrastructural capacity, and it identifies the sources that speak to a state's capacity to implement its goals. Specifically, social control refers to the kind of power through which the state translates its goals into goal-oriented action. This power is called social control because, as Migdal argues, the ability of the state to actually take goal-oriented action rests upon maintaining a political, legal, and normative order. The power that facilitates social control issues from three sources: penetration, extraction, and the regulation of social relations.

Penetration. Penetration is a way of describing the extent to which a state's authority is extended throughout society in a *nonrepressive* sense. Penetration is a source of social control and infrastructural capacity because it indicates the extent of state legitimacy. The degree to which a society regards its state as legitimate is crucial for effective national performance. Legitimacy is "the justification upon which authority is based and rule rendered 'rightful.'"[44] Although the state has coercive power over society, its ability to mobilize individuals and resources *efficiently* is much greater when society cooperates with the state rather than resisting it. When the state enjoys legitimacy, society tends to freely give the state authority to perform its crucial tasks like defense against external threat, maintenance of internal security, provision of collective goods, and supervision of the economy.[45]

---

[44]Timothy J. Lomperis, *From People's War to People's Rule: Insurgency, Intervention, and the Lessons of Vietnam* (Chapel Hill, N.C.: University of North Carolina Press, 1996), p. 5.

[45]Aaron Friedberg, "Why Didn't the United States Become a Garrison State?" *International Security*, Vol. 16 (Spring 1992), pp. 109–142.

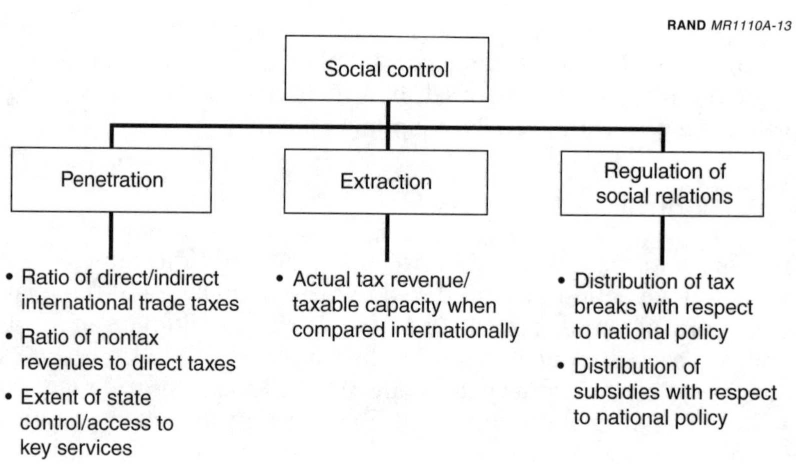

Figure 13—"Social Control" and Illustrative Indicators

The legitimacy of the state derives from two basic sources. First, there is the factor of performance. The state is in the business of providing society with two crucial collective goods: security from external threat and domestic security. States have also come to assume various welfare and economic functions. If the state does well at these tasks, it is likely to be accorded the presumption of legitimacy by society. However, if the state's legitimacy is based *solely* on performance, its legitimacy is hostage to performance failures. Hence, legitimacy based solely on performance is brittle and may not endure. The second, more securely rooted basis of legitimacy is normative. Legitimacy in this sense reflects the fact that the state has a moral authority to rule because the political arrangements it represents embody the values and interests held either universally within a country (that is, as Reinhard Bendix put it, a legitimate state is a form of "universal particularism"[46]) or by elites who through the

[46]For discussions of the concept of legitimacy, see Reinhard Bendix, *Kings or People: Power and the Mandate to Rule* (Berkeley: University of California Press, 1978); Max Weber (trans. and intro. by H. P. Secher), *Basic Concepts in Sociology* (Secaucus, NJ: Citadel Press, 1962); Dolf Sternbeger, "Legitimacy," in David L. Sills (gen. ed.), *International Encyclopedia of the Social Sciences*, Vol. 9 (New York: Crowell Collier and Macmillan, 1968).

"fabric of hegemony"[47] successfully create the foundations for universal consent to the domination of a particular class. The loss of legitimacy, or the lack thereof, does not mean the state will collapse. As Timothy J. Lomperis notes, the state can rule without legitimacy but cannot rule well: "If it has legitimacy, as challenges arise, a regime can invoke willing obedience, acts of loyalty, and deeds of self-sacrifice."[48]

For these reasons, any useful assessment of national power must account for the legitimacy of the state, and penetration is a useful inferential measure of legitimacy because it encodes the degree of a population's relative acceptance of the state. The state's penetration of society precedes and in fact makes possible its extraction of resources from society.[49] Penetration thus represents the dynamic interaction between the state and its population, and this relationship has been operationalized by one scholar in the following way:[50]

$$\text{PENETRATION} = \frac{\text{extension of state authority throughout society}}{\text{state susceptibility to external shocks}}$$

This formula is intended to convey the idea that both the extent of state authority and the extent of state flexibility must be incorporated into the notion of penetration, which ultimately derives from the density of the interface between the state and its population. Thus, the greater the proportion of people who directly interface with the state, the greater the degree of state penetration. From the perspective of measuring infrastructural capacity, *this is meant to imply that*

---

[47]This theme forms the intellectual foundation in Antonio Gramsci (ed. and intro. by Joseph A. Buttigieg; trans. Joseph A. Buttigieg and Antonio Callari), *Prison Notebooks*, vols. 1 and 2 (New York: Columbia University Press, 1992, 1996).

[48]Lomperis, op. cit., pp. 33, 55. As Skocpol notes, when the state lacks legitimacy, its ability to maintain itself with a degree of stability hinges on the ability of its coercive organizations to "remain coherent and effective." Theda Skocpol, *States and Social Revolutions: A Comparative Analysis of France, Russia, and China* (Cambridge: Cambridge University Press, 1979), p. 32.

[49]Lewis W. Snider, "Identifying the Elements of State Power: Where Do We Begin?" *Comparative Political Studies*, Vol. 20, No. 3 (1987), pp. 320–321, and "Comparing the Strength of Nations: The Arab Gulf States and Political Change," *Comparative Politics* (July 1988), p. 467.

[50]Snider, op. cit. (1987), p. 327.

greater state penetration results in greater social control, which in turn represents an enhanced ability to implement goal-directed action, which finally results in a greater capacity to augment national power.

How can penetration in these senses be evaluated? In principle, it can be evaluated by measures that capture the extent of direct interaction between governments and society. This can be either through formal bureaucratic rational-legal institutions or through autocratic forms of government where the discretionary power of the executive is based heavily on interpersonal claims. In any event, the *manner* in which a state raises its financial resources becomes the best indicator of its level of penetration vis-à-vis society. As Skocpol argues, "a state's means of raising and deploying financial resources tells us more than could any other single factor about its existing (and immediately potential) capacities to create or strengthen state organizations, to employ personnel, to coopt political support, to subsidize economic enterprises, and to fund social programs."[51]

Empirical studies have suggested several different measures of penetration, all linked by their common focus on the state's fiscal powers vis-à-vis society. In countries that have legal-rational institutions, the ratio of taxes on international trade and foreign transactions as a percentage of total government revenue has been identified as the most useful indicator of authority because, as Snider puts it, "direct taxes are relatively more difficult to collect than indirect taxes because they require more effective infrastructural power. Taxes on international trade and transactions are the easiest to levy because relatively little infrastructural power is needed to collect them."[52] This logic suggests a second related measure of penetration, namely, the ratio of direct to indirect taxes in a given country. Both measures together would indicate the extent of state strength: strong states, that is, states with greater authority, should be able to collect a higher level of taxes from direct levies domestically as opposed to weaker

[51]Skocpol, "Bringing the State Back In," p. 17.

[52]Snider, op. cit. (1987), pp. 325–326.

states, which would rely more on trade and indirect taxes as a percentage of total revenue.[53]

While the structure of taxation provides a useful indicator of the extension of state power throughout society, the state's susceptibility to external shocks (which is another element of penetration) requires another type of measure, though also one derived from the tax system. This measure of flexibility consists of examining the ratio of nontax revenues to the taxes on international trade and transactions or even more simply as the ratio of nontax revenues to indirect taxes. Such a measure is necessary because the greater the proportion of taxes coming from international trade, the greater a state's susceptibility to shocks emanating from the international system. In such a situation, the flexibility enjoyed by the state can be captured by the extent of its domestic nontax revenues which would allow state managers to buffer society against the negative effects of external shocks. Focusing on nontax revenues also provides the additional benefit of having an indicator of penetration that is more suited to countries which, lacking bureaucratic structures of the legal-rational kind, are managed by more or less autocratic forms of government. The extent of nontax revenues here measures "the wider discretionary flexibility"[54] associated with such forms of government by providing "an indication of [such] governments to provide services to their population [or to pursue other national goals] in the face of their susceptibility to external pressures."[55] Stronger states, understood as states with greater flexibility, would therefore have a higher percentage of nontax revenues to international trade revenues or indirect taxes in comparison to weaker states.

Extraction. Extraction is another crucial manifestation of social control. It is a measure of the state's ability to gain the resources it needs to achieve its goals through the labor, participation, and cooperation of society. In a different way it too is a measure of legitimacy, but its importance here derives primarily from its being a critical

---

[53]This is because, as Snider notes, "direct taxes require a more developed capacity to make the state's presence felt in the event of noncompliance than other forms." Snider, op. cit. (1987), p. 328.

[54]Ibid.

[55]Ibid.

measure of the state's ability to garner societal wealth in the context of pursuing national power, particularly as evidenced by its commitment to produce, first, those intermediate goods necessary for the creation of actionable knowledge and, finally, the military instruments that enable a country to dominate in the arena of international politics. As Kugler and Domke have argued,

> The most capable [states] extract and allocate a larger portion of available resources for war purposes. Accordingly, analyzing the flow of revenues from the societal to the [state] resource pool provides an effective measurement of the political component of power . . . [particularly because the evidence suggests that] . . . the [usual] winners of war are those who have the resources and the political capacity to mobilize and maintain a war effort.[56]

The ability of a state to extract the wealth it needs from society, thus, turns out to be an important component of its ability to attain certain political goals because, other things being equal, the greater the extractive capacity, the greater the state's ability to pursue the acquisition of the most modern military instruments available. At a preliminary level, therefore, the argument about the relationship between extraction and infrastructural capability might be said to take the following form: *greater extractive capacity makes for greater social control, which in turn reflects a greater ability to implement goal-oriented action, which finally produces greater levels of national power.*

How can the state's capacity for extraction be measured? The best measure derives from the fiscal system, this time focused on the level of revenue rather than on the character of the tax structure. As Snider argues,

> Taxes are a direct indicator of government presences. Few government activities impinge upon the lives of most members of society or depend as heavily on popular support or fear of punishment as taxation. Very few government operations are pursued as relentlessly or avoided as vigorously. The differentials in energy that governments must exert to collect taxes from societies with comparable

---

[56]Kugler and Domke, "Comparing the Strength of Nations," op. cit., p. 42.

> resource bases is one observable manifestation of a state's attempts to implement its own objectives against resistance from society.[57]

For that reason, Kugler and Domke and others have focused on developing various measures of a state's political capacity for extraction that, without all the refinements, essentially boil down to the ratio of the revenues a state actually extracts divided by the predicted values of what it could extract *compared to other states with a similar resource base*. Establishing such a benchmark does not require measuring the extractive capability of all comparably situated countries: rather, a small sample of the most important countries enjoying comparable GNP, or a small sample that includes the most important competitors or rivals of the country in question, ought to suffice.

This indicator, it must be noted, is essentially a comparative indicator between countries. Such a comparative indicator is essential because, contrary to the preliminary argument offered earlier, extremely high levels of extraction via taxes can be achieved only at the price of both losing the flexibility to raise revenues further and, more important, creating deleterious economic consequences that ensue when states appropriate *too great a share* of societal wealth. If the latter in fact occurs, the national economy may actually be weakened as high tax burdens stifle private innovation, investment, and entrepreneurship. In some circumstances, therefore, a country could become less powerful externally to the degree that the internal extractive capacity of the state actually increases. To accommodate this phenomenon of diminishing returns to increasing extraction (among others), there can be no unique measure of desirable extraction, simply comparative measures of how efficient some states are relative to others in the same (or similar) income category. For the same reason, the levels of penetration and extraction must be measured simultaneously, because decreasing penetration in the face of increasing extraction may actually indicate an incipient legitimacy problem that may eventually decrease the infrastructural power of the state.

Regulation of social relations. The final locus of social control is the ability of the state to regulate social relations. The way or extent to

---

[57]Snider, "Comparing the Strength of Nations," op. cit., p. 466.

which a state can control the relationships between members of its society will become a source of infrastructural power by providing a state with the leverage to prevent its goals from becoming proxy to special interests. This dynamic between state and society taps into a source of power that penetration and extraction do not. Whereas penetration is a dynamic between state and society indicating whether a state is legitimate enough to define societal goals, and extraction is a dynamic between state and society indicating the ability of the former to translate legitimacy into real actions oriented toward carrying out certain policies that promise to increase national power, the regulation of social relations represents a dynamic between state and society that indicates the ability of the state *to control the agenda once goal-oriented action has been implemented.* The regulation of social relations thus functions as a gauge of the state's ability to achieve the goals it has sought.

The regulation of social relations is an important aspect of social control because state policies could still be subverted even *after* the state effectively sets its goals and acquires the necessary resources—both in terms of legitimacy and wealth—to pursue them. Such subversion could occur thanks to the intervention of various special interest groups that attempt to appropriate the extracted resources in a manner other than the one the state had intended. Some goal may thus be eventually attained, but perhaps not the one that had been intended, set, and pursued by the state. The infrastructural capacity of the state, therefore, is also affected by the struggle for control between state organs and various powerful social groups. For this reason, the state's capacity to regulate the social relations within the realm must also be assessed as a part of the scrutiny of its infrastructural capacity, and Migdal has suggested that the most appropriate measure here is one that centers on the ability of the state to compel citizens to follow its rules and participate in state-sanctioned institutions. In operationalizing this principle, Migdal himself suggests measuring the number of voters as a percentage of society, the level of school enrollment, or the known or acknowledged instances of bribery in public life.

While the general principle is appropriate, the measures of social regulation suggested by Migdal are problematic because, as he himself acknowledges, such indicators tend to measure penetration much more than social relationships. For example, he points out that it does little good in assessing regulation of social relations to know that a state has a huge number of police or military personnel on its payroll, since the state's level of coherence may be so low that most security officers effectively take their orders from outside it, from those with rules quite different from the ones espoused by state leaders. Also, a number of indicators suggested by him do not distinguish effectively between social and material resources: for example, population size, GDP, and state abilities to extract or employ those resources. Consequently, he suggests school enrollment data because it reflects the variability of states in using control to mobilize the population into participating in state institutions and rules.

These measures should be amended, however, to capture a single reality: How successfully has the state enrolled people in carrying out its proclaimed missions? This implies that the best test might be one that measures the coherence between the declared policy of the state and the orientation of its fiscal instruments. More specifically, testing for the "fit" between the pattern of tax breaks, subsidies, and penalties with respect to national policy provides a good indication of how powerful the state may be vis-à-vis powerful social groups (including those that might support the state) *after certain national goals are framed and the resources collected to pursue them.* Tax breaks, subsidies, and penalties that are at variance with the proclaimed objectives of the state would suggest that state organs are in fact hostage to powerful special interests. That is, no matter how well they can articulate their interests and garner the resources necessary to pursue those interests, they still have some difficulty in implementing their preferred course of action at the level of actual policy.

There is no doubt that articulating these interests itself is the product of societal pressure, but that is something that normally occurs in the process of goal-setting or what this framework has termed "self-control." The notion of regulating social relations, however, attempts to measure whether a state—after having articulated its interests—can still keep them from being subverted by coalitions that may have an interest in frustrating their execution. The argument here, then, is intended to suggest that *greater regulative capacity on the part of the state results in increased capacity for social control, which in turn results in an increased ability to implement goal-oriented action, which finally results in a high ability to augment national power.*

IDEATIONAL RESOURCES

The infrastructural capability of the state represents an important component of national performance. That is, the state's ability to penetrate society, extract resources from society, and regulate social relations within society all interact to determine whether it can adequately respond to the pressures to dominate emerging from the international system. Infrastructural capability, however, simply describes the *material* components necessary for an adequate state response to the issue of national power. It does not describe whether the state will be able to convert its control over society into both resources, which are the intermediate goods or "inputs," and effective military capabilities, which are the "outputs" or ultimate manifestations of national power. Accomplishing this conversion process adequately requires an additional element—ideational resources—and this element, which represents the third dimension of the transformative level, refers to the capacity for both instrumental and substantive rationality. Ideational resources, consequently, are "intangible capabilities" that derive from the "problem-solving" ability and the "value system" of a given country; unlike infrastructural capability, which emerges from the dynamics *between* state and society, ideational resources remain a characteristic of the polity taken as a whole.

Although the source of a country's "problem-solving" ability and "value system" cannot be discerned in any essentialist sense, it is possible to argue that ideational resources are for practical purposes constituted by the interaction of state, society, and the international system. Structural constraints emanating from the international system generally impel states to maximize their power, which in turn should condition state managers—through instrumental reason—to place a premium on the pursuit of national wealth and military capability.[58] Whether the state managers actually do so, however,

---

[58]See, for example, Gilpin, *War and Change in World Politics;* Kennedy, *The Rise and Fall of the Great Powers;* Tilly, *Coercion, Capital, and European States;* and Layne, "The Unipolar Illusion."

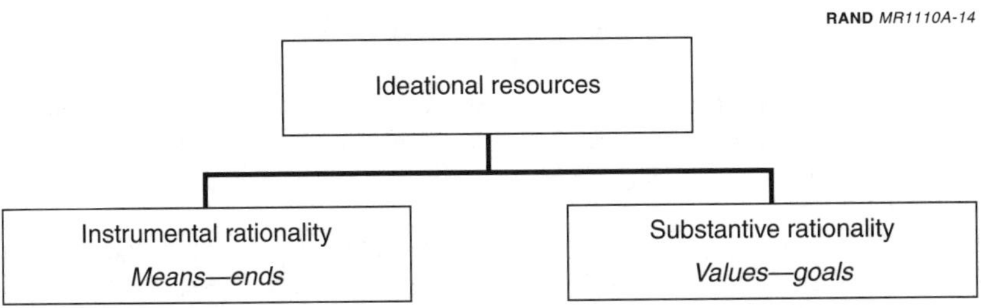

Figure 14—Understanding Ideational Resources

hinges in part on "the availability and (even more problematically) the appropriate use of sound ideas about what the state can and should do to address [political] problems."[59] Further, whether the state has the organizational structures to act on these ideas becomes equally relevant: in fact, the proof of substantive rationality at the national level will often be found in "the fit (or lack thereof) between the scope of an autonomous state organization's authority and the scale and depth of action appropriate for addressing a given kind of problem."[60]

The issue of whether a country possesses the requisite ideational resources for the production of national power then boils down to whether it is objectively well adapted to the goals that it must attain if it is to both survive and flourish in the international system. As illustrated in Figure 14, this concern, in turn, can be decomposed into two broad questions: (i) Does the country exhibit a high level of instrumental rationality, understood as the ability to adequately relate means to ends? This question can be examined at the level of both elite and mass, but a scrutiny at the latter level is more productive here because it captures the "problem-solving" orientation of the populace as a whole rather than the capability of any privileged subgroup within the country. (ii) Does the country exhibit a high level of substantive rationality, understood as a *national* commitment to the pursuit of wealth and the acquisition of power? This characterization of substantive rationality derives directly from the

---

[59]Skocpol, "Bringing the State Back In," p. 15.

[60]Ibid.

constraints imposed by the international system on any given country, and it allows for a scrutiny of both the instrumental rationality of elites as evidenced through the organizational structure of the state and the incentives it offers as well as the character of state ideology and the nature of societal organization within a country.

The answers to these two questions are clearly important because of their substantive effect on the pursuit of national power. As Heyman suggests, certain kinds of problem-solving "thoughtwork" are better suited to certain goals than others. It is in this transition from a mental disposition and a guideline for setting goals and responding to opportunity, obstacles, and ambiguity that the problem-solving orientation and the value system of a country becomes a resource that matters for the potential to enhance national power. Both instrumental rationality understood as problem-solving orientation and substantive rationality understood as the value system of a country will therefore be analyzed in turn.

Instrumental Rationality

If instrumental rationality is considered as an ideational resource that is valuable for the production of national power, it becomes relevant at three different levels of decisionmaking. At the first-order level, it forces decisionmaking entities, be they individuals or states, to answer the question, "What is to be done?" To answer this question, this level of instrumental rationality confronts actors with the need to define the *objectives* they wish to pursue from among the infinite possibilities facing any entity at a given point in time. The choice of objectives here will be conditioned both by the situational constraints facing the agent as well as the agent's own preferences, irrespective of where they may be rooted. At the purely instrumental level of rationality, the reason for choosing one objective over another is irrelevant. All that is required is that the agent choose one goal from among the myriad alternatives and pursue it more or less consistently.

Once this first-order question is satisfactorily addressed, the second-order level of instrumental rationality interjects itself: this consists of compelling decisionmaking entities to answer the question, "How is it to be done?" Answering this question has both logical and empirical components. The logical component simply seeks to ensure that

RAND *MR1110A-15*

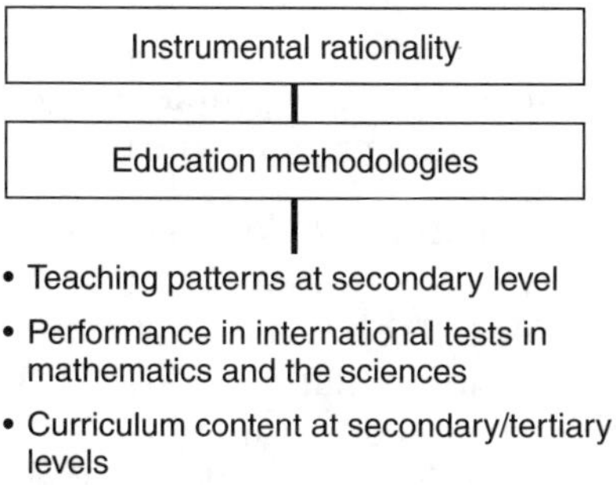

Figure 15—Instrumental Rationality and Illustrative Indicators

agents understand the "grammar" of their situation and act accordingly, whereas the empirical component requires agents to become aware of the numerous substantive components that define the difference between an inadequate and an adequate response to their situation: these include understanding the material constraints that may be facing the agent, the kinds of technical knowledge that may be required to address the problem, and the possible need for specific implements essential to the task at hand. This second level of instrumental rationality—which forces entities to answer the "How is it to be done?" question—invariably confronts agents with the fact that any rational response may involve alternative pathways that arise because the available means to even certain ends are afflicted by uncertainties and constraints of various kinds.

Consequently, the third-order level of instrumental rationality appears at this juncture, and this involves forcing decisionmaking entities to answer the question, "Which is the dominant solution?" Addressing this issue requires agents to identify the various alternative solutions predicated by the question "How is it to be done?" and rank order them after their multiple ambiguities and tradeoffs are delineated. When these ambiguities and tradeoffs are assessed in the light of the agent's own available and potential resources, his attitudes to risk, and the consequences of potential counteractions by others, some decision paths may turn out to be more attractive than others. In such circumstances, it may even be possible to find one decision path or solution—"the dominant solution"—that outranks all others either in terms of the expected benefits it promises or the depth of risk it minimizes. In other circumstances, dominant solutions may be unavailable, as the problem in question may not be "strictly determined" in the sense of game theory.

Whether or not a problem has a dominant solution, the three-step process associated with instrumental rationality remains a critical resource for being able to "solve" any problem, including ones associated with the production of national power. Because this process, in different forms, came to constitute the core of the Western scientific and intellectual tradition, it has allowed Western states and societies to derive enormous advantages in the production of national power. This is because it remains not only the best embodiment of universal reason—so far—but also happens to personify the most efficient path to modernity, and to technological progress in particular: by allowing for "the slow boring of hard boards"[61] it has, if political history since 1500 AD is any indication, made possible the kind of sustained, purposeful activity that can confront obstacles and undertake acts of transformation in the world.

The first issue, from the perspective of analyzing the ideational resources that make for national power, then consists of assessing the extent to which any country exhibits the kind of "methodical thinking"[62] that makes effective problem solving and political rationalization possible. The best evidence for such a phenomenon at the national level will be found in the institutions of socialization that involve mass education. It is at this level that the emphasis placed by the polity on the acquisition and transmission of methodical thinking, especially in the form of an effective problem-solving orientation, can be best discerned. Accordingly, the most useful indicators of embedded instrumental rationality will be found in the school system, particularly at the secondary level. If a national-level assessment is desired, however, it is important first to acquire data on enrollment and attainment rates, especially at the secondary level. The secondary level is critical because primary education con-

---

[61]Max Weber, *From Max Weber* (New York: Oxford University Press, 1946), p. 128.

[62]The phrase is Mary Dietz's and comes from her article, "The Slow Boring of Hard Boards: Methodical Thinking and the Work of Politics," *American Political Science Review*, Vol. 88, No. 4 (December 1994), pp. 873–886.

sists mainly of transmitting knowledge rather than training individuals in the art of problem solving associated with the notion of methodical thinking. Problem solving no doubt takes place consistently at the tertiary level, but tertiary education is generally relatively exclusive and is for the most part available to a relatively small fraction of the overall population. Consequently, enrollment and attainment rates at the secondary level provide the best quantitative indicators about the extent of the opportunities available for transmitting the techniques of methodical thinking within a country. Lower enrollment and attainment rates would suggest lesser exposure to the instruments of rationalization, while higher rates would suggest just the opposite.

Besides the enrollment and attainment rates at the secondary level, however, other more specific indicators are required. These consist primarily of three variables: teaching methodology, curriculum time, and nature of national examinations. The indicators relating to teaching methodology should focus on assessing whether the mode of instruction emphasizes the acquisition of received wisdom in the form of "facts" or focuses on inculcating problem-solving techniques and encouraging creativity in general. The indicators relating to curriculum time should focus on assessing the time spent on science and mathematics relative to other subjects in the curriculum, on the premise that science and mathematics represent the problem-solving disciplines par excellence. The indicators relating to the national examination system should focus on assessing whether the national examinations place a premium on regurgitating facts or whether they emphasize analysis and creativity. It is possible that little international data exists on these variables. If so, such assessments will have to rely mainly on expert appraisal or reputational evaluations, limited though they may be as methods of assessment. Evaluating the level of embedded instrumental rationality in a country is a tricky exercise at the best of times, and therefore the indicators suggested above must be viewed mainly as a "first cut" at this difficult problem.

Substantive Rationality

The second dimension of ideational resources consists of substantive rationality. Issues of substantive rationality are generally avoided by social scientists because the fact-value distinction and the notion of

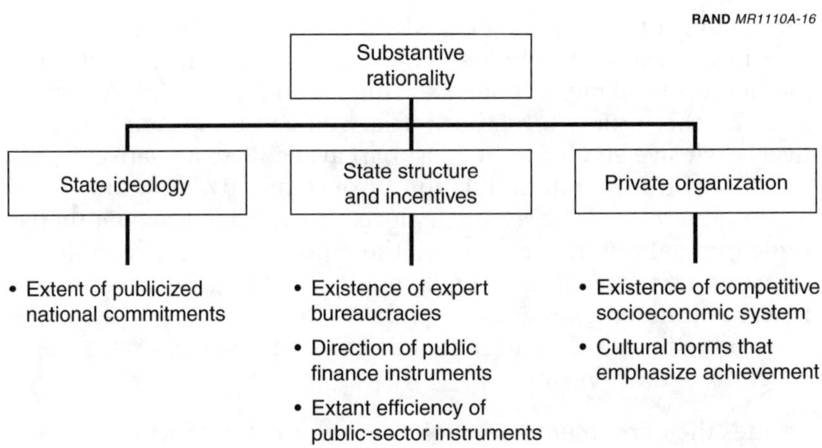

Figure 16—Substantive Rationality and Illustrative Indicators

value neutrality together are often presumed to require an abdication of judgment with respect to the ends pursued by any decision-making entity. Fortunately, this problem can be avoided entirely here because the nature of the external pressures described earlier clearly suggest what is substantively rational for any country in the international system: pursuing a corporatist commitment to the production of wealth and power so as to be able to respond successfully to the structural constraints to dominate in international politics. The necessity to engage in an evaluation of rationality in general and substantive rationality in particular is also motivated by the desire to capture an unregulated source of transformation that is not easy to characterize and is not accounted for by either infrastructural power or external constraints.

Consider, for example, a state that has strong infrastructural power and is buffeted by international conditions that would lead it to develop both a strong resource base and a powerful military, yet fails to do so. In such a situation, what is likely to have happened is that in spite of favorable internal and external dynamics, the state may simply have a set of goals that don't cohere with the power required by the international system, especially as manifested in the post-industrial age. It may possess instrumental rationality because that is, at least at some level, a calculative ability natural to all human beings and social organizations (to the degree that the latter are composed of rational agents). But it may not possess substantive rationality understood as a corporate commitment to the production of wealth and power, either because it is dominated by insular and rapacious elites, or because it possesses otiose decisionmaking organs, or because it is supported by a cultural framework that is either indifferent to, or does not actively support, national power expansion. If such a country exists, it is possible to argue that its failure to ultimately develop national power is rooted not in the absence of international pressures or infrastructural power but rather in the weakness of its ideational resources, particularly as manifested in the realm of substantive rationality.

As Amilcar Herrera has demonstrated in the context of his inquiry into why states with equal resources have had variable success in building a productive high-technology economy, the intellectual model of society to which elites overtly or implicitly subscribe affect how science and technology, for example, have developed.[63] The importance of ideational resources, particularly in the form of substantive rationality, thus becomes clear in the case of Latin America, where enormous amounts of aid and skills contributed by international organizations and the industrialized countries for science and technology development produced, after three decades of sustained effort, little in terms of movement toward developing modern, capable, scientific societies.[64] So unless this dimension is included in the account of national performance, the intangible resources that affect the production of inputs and their transformation into military capability will escape analysis.

Understanding the extent of substantive rationality within a country, therefore, requires an assessment of how closely national organizations comport to the ideal of power- and progress-oriented rationality and how effectively they embody a "conscious human effort to enlarge material power."[65] The objective here is to discern whether

---

[63]Amilcar Herrera, "Social Determinants of Science Policy in Latin America: Explicit Science Policy and Implicit Science Policy," in Charles Cooper (ed.), *Science, Technology and Development* (Frank Cass: London, 1973), p. 19.

[64]Op. cit., pp. 19–20.

[65]Hannah Arendt, *The Human Condition* (Chicago: University of Chicago Press, 1958), p. 52.

countries have institutions and structures that allow them to pursue processes relevant to the production of national power:

- institutions which can define the basic objectives of state managers;
- institutions which can define criteria of choice to translate the basic objectives into an objective function to be used operationally for choosing the optimum technology and technique;
- institutions which can define the preparation of a menu of technological and technical alternatives;
- institutions which can identify and respond to the objective conditions that constrain or facilitate the choices made by planners.[66]

Not surprisingly, the role of the state turns out to be critical in this regard, and it often requires state managers to intrude upon the activities of "civil society."[67] The state must be able to set goals, obtain the resources to achieve those goals, and encourage nonstate actors in society (for example, business enterprises, social classes) to cooperate in the attainment of the state's aims. Obviously, the degree of state intrusiveness will vary depending on the nature of the country's economic and political systems. The sphere of state control is less in a liberal democratic market system than in a nondemocratic command economy. Nevertheless, even in liberal democratic market economies, the state's role is much greater than is commonly thought. As Robert Gilpin has pointed out, even in market economies the state has a broad array of instruments it can use to directly and indirectly affect the behavior of social actors. Some of these instruments are monetary policy, tax policy, fiscal policy, building of communications and transportation infrastructure, support for education, and subsidization of research and development.[68]

---

[66]This framework is inspired by the discussion in Shigeru Ishikawa, "A Note on the Choice of Technology in China," in Cooper, op. cit., p. 162.

[67]The discussion in the following paragraphs is based on Rueschemeyer and Evans, "The State and Economic Transformation."

[68]Robert Gilpin, *The Political Economy of International Relations* (Princeton: Princeton University Press, 1987).

The state's role is to set goals and priorities, and to commit the resources needed to implement its policies. And it needs to communicate these goals and priorities to, and gain assent from, society. The state has the task of creating the assumptions and expectations that will serve as the basis for a common effort throughout society. The state uses legal constraints and material inducements to impose on society its concept of substantive rationality. To be maximally effective, these legal constraints and material inducements need to be institutionalized in state organizations. Thus, the keys to developing substantively rational policies and norms with respect to the state's pursuit of wealth and power are to be found in the state's bureaucratic-administrative apparatus and legal system.

Though simply stated, the dynamics of substantive rationality are actually subtle, because they involve a dialectical process between the state and society. The state, in the first instance, sets the attainment of wealth and power as its preeminent policy objective and through ideological organs seeks to mobilize national support in pursuit of this objective. The first indicator of substantive rationality, therefore, would be state ideology or evidence of a deliberate, public commitment to the production of wealth and power, particularly in the form of acquiring modern science and technology. Having formulated this objective, however, the state cannot by itself generate the economic and technological resources to achieve its desired ends. These resources are generated by other social actors (firms, entrepreneurs, research laboratories, individuals, etc.) but guided by the state whenever necessary. Occasionally, the state itself will undertake such resource-generation activities, especially in areas critical to national security. The second indicator of substantive rationality, therefore, is the existence of a state structure oriented to the production of wealth and power: this would be manifested by (i) the existence of expert bureaucracies that identify the desired capabilities sought by the state; (ii) the routine use of public finance instruments, especially the national budget, to procure, subsidize, or provide incentives for the production of desired capabilities; and (iii) the existence of public-sector undertakings aimed at directly producing capabilities otherwise beyond the capabilities of civil society. Beyond motivating societal actors and occasionally substituting for them, the state must use its institutionalized powers of coercion and persuasion to cause social actors in general to behave in ways that will create the means the state requires to achieve its ends, and this may include both creating and sustaining a competitive socioeconomic system as well as manipulating cultural norms to emphasize personal achievement. This is not an easy task. And states that have the infrastructural power to generate effective military capabilities may nevertheless fail because they lack the institutionalized, bureaucratic machinery to impose a coherence at the level of substantive rationality on society. In any event, the third indicator of substantive rationality would therefore be the existence of a competitive socioeconomic system and the prevalence of cultural norms that emphasize achievement. The former would include, for example, the existence of institutions that preserve private property rights, enable effective nonviolent dispute resolution, and provide sufficient public safety and political order.

Chapter Seven

MEASURING MILITARY CAPABILITY

The ultimate yardstick of national power is military capability. Because countries subsist in an environment where internal and external threats to security are both common and ever-present, the effectiveness of their coercive arms becomes the ultimate measure of power. Military capabilities allow countries to defend themselves against all adversaries, foreign and domestic, while simultaneously enabling their state managers to pursue whatever interests they wish, if necessary over and against the preferences of other competing entities. As Peter Paret summarized it, "military power expresses and implements the power of the state in a variety of ways within and beyond the state borders, and is also one of the instruments with which political power is originally created and made permanent."[1] For this reason, the ultimate "output" of national power should be—ideally—the ability of a military force to successfully prosecute a variety of operations against a country's adversaries. Whether a force is in fact capable of overwhelming these adversaries requires a detailed analysis of the balance of power, the circumstances under which the engagement occurs, and the relevant constraints and objectives that condition the overall interaction between the two sides. This effort often requires dynamic combat analysis, including simulations and gaming, to determine the *relative* balance of effectiveness between any two forces.

[1]Peter Paret, "Military Power," *The Journal of Military History,* Vol. 53, No. 3 (July 1989), p. 240.

Besides the practical difficulties attending such work, detailed analysis of this sort will not be undertaken here, mainly for methodological reasons: since the objective is not to assess power as an "outcome" but only as a "resource," measuring military capability here will focus mainly on understanding which ingredients are necessary for the creation of an effective force and how the effectiveness of this force can be conceptualized in an intellectual sense. The measures of military capability suggested here, therefore, remain "input measures"[2] in the specific sense used by Stephen Biddle: they focus on understanding what "goes into" the making of an effective national military capability and how such effectiveness can be compared across countries in a comparative-static sense without either doing any military balance analysis or pretending that it can explain how any given force-on-force encounters will actually turn out in practice. In that sense, the framework in this chapter is intended to be a *prelude* to dynamic combat analysis, but emphatically not a substitute for it.

The notion of military capability as the output level of national power is premised on the understanding that a country's military organizations receive national resources and transform them into specific warfighting capabilities. The warfighting capabilities thus generated are effective to the degree that they enable a country's leaders to impose their will on enemies, existing and potential. Thus, the larger logical framework developed for examining national power can be applied writ small to examining how national military establishments generate effective military forces. Put simply, the question is, "What resources does the military get, and how successfully can they be transformed into effective military power?" Military effectiveness thus becomes the outcome of the resources provided to the military and its capability to transform these resources into effective warfighting capability. A country may provide its military with generous budgets and large cadres of manpower, but if the military's doctrine is misguided, the training ineffective, the leadership unschooled, or the organization inappropriate, military capability will suffer.

---

[2]Stephen D. Biddle, "The European Conventional Balance: A Reinterpretation of the Debate," *Survival,* Vol. 30, No. 2 (March–April 1988), pp. 99–121.

The problems of measuring military capability are, in many respects, quite similar to the difficulties faced in measuring national power. Certainly one or two individual measures—the number of personnel under arms, for example, or the number of tanks or missile launchers in a nation's inventory—are unlikely to capture the key factors for assessing military power, just as a single measure does not provide a useful assessment of a country's overall power. A single measure may be useful for ranking states by particular dimensions of military capability, but it will not capture more than a small part of the variance in the effectiveness of military forces. It is obvious, for example, that the largest armies may not necessarily be the most effective. In the 1960s and 1970s, Israel's small forces defeated larger opponents. The People's Liberation Army is numerically the largest military in the world, but today China cannot project significant power beyond its borders. The capability of a military force, therefore, depends on more than just the resources made available to the coercive arms of the state. Consider, for example, the contrast in the military capabilities of Israel and New Zealand. Both have modern economies, well-educated populations, access to world markets and modern technologies, and freely elected governments. Yet their armed forces are quite different. Though their resources are significantly different (Israel's GDP is twice that of New Zealand), Israel is directly threatened by nearby neighbors and defends itself without formal allies. New Zealand is an island nation, faces no apparent external threats, and is allied with Australia and the United States. So military threats, geography, and alliances also help shape a country's force architecture and, ultimately, its effective military capabilities.

The framework for examining military capability as the output dimension of national power is patterned analogously to the larger framework for assessing national power. It seeks to identify the strategic resources a military receives from the government it serves; the variables bearing upon the means by which these resources are converted into effective capabilities; and, finally, the capabilities of the combat force itself understood via a spectrum of warfighting competencies that may be attained to a greater or lesser degree and which may be compared across countries.

STRATEGIC RESOURCES

Any consideration of a country's military capabilities or its military effectiveness must begin with an examination of the resources—financial, human, physical, and technological—that the national leadership makes available to its military organizations. These resources are clearly a function of the larger national-level assets possessed by a country (examined earlier under the rubric of "national resources") as well as the imperatives emerging from national performance, that is, the pressures levied by external threats, the power of the state vis-à-vis its society, and the ideational acuity with which both state managers and society as a whole can perceive problems and develop satisfactory solutions. These two dimensions, operating interactively, then define the kind of resources transferred to the military; any analysis that seeks to measure national power in military terms, especially in the context of a country's ability to undertake the "information-dominant" operations that are seen to revolutionize warfare, must gather and assess information pertaining to the following variables.

Defense Budgets

The size of the defense budget is, in principle, the most general single measure of the resources provided to a military by its political masters. The size of the defense budget serves to identify the relative importance of the coercive arm in comparison to other organs of state, and it conveys a general sense of the size of the military establishment in absolute terms. Toward that end, data revealing the size of the defense budget as a percentage of both overall public spending and of GDP/GNP are essential. In addition, however, these macro-indices should be refined by an analysis of the internal heads of account. Specifically, understanding the distribution of resources among the various services provides a preliminary view of a country's understanding of the salience of relative threats, its desired structure of combat proficiency, as well as the relative power of various military bureaucracies. Similarly, understanding the patterns of disbursement in functional terms, that is, with respect to pay and allowances, operations and maintenance, force procurement, and research and development, also provides critical information about a country's military power. When such data are aggregated in the form

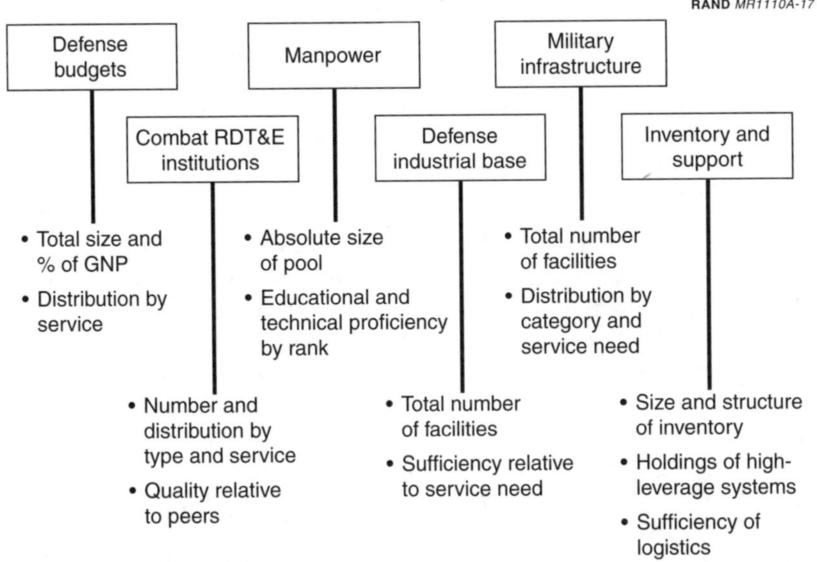

Figure 17—Strategic Resources and Illustrative Indicators

of a time series, they identify important trends as far as changes in national military effectiveness are concerned. The defense budget of a country can be analyzed in multiple ways, but an analysis that focuses on understanding the character of national military capabilities must assess budgetary allocations and movements in terms of the disbursement of resources among combat forces, support and maintenance, operational and physical infrastructure, and defense management and command accounts.[3] In many countries, however, budgetary data at such a high level of disaggregation and specificity may be unavailable. So analysis and estimation is required. Analysis of military budgets in this instance may require examining the observable physical resources possessed by a given military and then working "backward" to compute their costs to the national

[3]For a revealing analysis of the value of such a breakup, see Kevin Lewis, "The Discipline Gap and Other Reasons for Humility and Realism in Defense Planning," in Paul K. Davis (ed.), *New Challenges for Defense Planning* (Santa Monica, CA: RAND, 1994), pp. 101–132.

exchequer. While such assessments are always less than precise, they are nonetheless valuable as broad yardsticks for assessing a state's commitment to its coercive arms and as such remain a crucial first step for measuring the outputs of national power.

Manpower

The size and quality of military manpower is the second kind of resource that yields insight into a country's national power. Very obviously, the size of a military force is important, first, as a crude index of military strength, and second, because quantity has a quality all its own in many, still relevant, combat environments. As a first cut, therefore, measures of military strength, which focus on examining the size of the total force, the breakup between active and reserve components, and the distribution of numbers across the services, would yield useful information that depicts, if nothing else, at least the relative mass of raw power that a country could bring to bear in some warfighting situations. In an era increasingly defined by information-intensive means of war, however, the most useful information about military manpower consists of data relating to qualitative variables: in particular, the educational levels of both the officer corps and the enlisted ranks and the levels of technical proficiency demanded of the recruiting base would provide critical information about the ability of a given military force to integrate and exploit the kind of sophisticated military technologies now being diffused throughout the international system. In this connection, data about force management issues within the military would also be very illuminating: whether a regimental tradition or its equivalent exists; whether national societal divisions are reflected or attenuated in the military sphere; whether issues of integration by gender, class, race, or ethnicity are salient in the force. All such information—quantitative whenever possible, qualitative whenever necessary—contributes toward evaluating the character of the military manpower pool and its potential effectiveness in conflict.

Military Infrastructure

The extent and quality of military infrastructure is the third kind of resource that has an impact on the quality of military capability. This category subsumes the physical infrastructure possessed by a military force, normally labeled "bases and installations." In addition to the facilities normally used to house military personnel and their equipment, this category should assess the number and quality of test and training ranges, medical facilities, military construction projects, and the like. Since military infrastructure must ultimately be assessed by its ability to support the warfighter, quality assessments ultimately become part and parcel of the analysis: thus, for example, when examining air warfare capabilities, analysis pertaining to the number of bases relative to the size of the air force will also incorporate more detailed examination about the kind of protection offered to aircraft, the mix between active and passive protection, the degree of hardness embodied by the shelters, and the survivability of crucial assets like command, control, and communications (C^3), petroleum, oil, and lubricants (POL), and munitions. While all these resources can be conceived of as constituting part of the military capital stocks of a given country (and, by implication, a contributor to military effectiveness), their value from the perspective of measuring national power derives from additional considerations that involve not simply data collection but also analytical judgment. Two questions become particularly pertinent in this regard: Does the country in question have the necessary number and range of facilities and installations to adequately train its military personnel in the combat and combat support tasks facing the force? Is the quality of these facilities comparable to those in the country's peer competitors and/or the United States?

Combat RDT&E Institutions

The number and quality of combat research institutions is the fourth kind of resource that affects military capability. The rapid transformations in both technology and the military arts have resulted in a need for increasingly specialized institutions that focus on research, development, test, and evaluation (RDT&E) activities relating to combat. These institutions could be: academic institutions, which specialize in training soldiers in the history of war or the higher requirements of command; specialized establishments, which focus on honing certain specific warfighting skills; technical centers, which either develop, test, and evaluate new equipment for various combat elements or advance new concepts of operations for military technologies developed by other institutions; or research organizations, which focus on studying foreign military forces and their organization, equipment, patterns of training, and doctrine. The presence of a large number of such institutions provides an important clue to the professionalism of a country's military force and the relative emphasis laid on solving certain strategic or operational challenges and learning from others. As with the issue of military infrastructure considered earlier, the value of the combat RDT&E institutions from the perspective of measuring national power derives from the intelligence community's ability to discern, first, whether the target country has the necessary number and range of institutions to adequately support its military forces in their operational tasks, and second, whether the quality of these institutions is comparable to those in the country's peer competitors and/or the United States.

Defense Industrial Base

The structure, extent, and quality of a country's defense industrial base constitutes the fifth kind of resource affecting military effectiveness. The defense industrial base essentially consists of firms or industries that depend on a country's defense spending for survival and upon which the country itself depends for the production of military technologies and instruments. Understanding the structure and quality of the defense industrial base allows the intelligence community to assess the quality of the military instruments domestically available to a country's military forces while simultaneously discerning its degree of dependence on others. The latter issue is particularly relevant from the viewpoint of understanding a country's potential vulnerabilities in the context of conflict. One generic approach to assessing the defense industrial base would be to classify by quality and the degree of self-sufficiency a country's ability to produce: large and small weapons; nonlethal but strategic products; and supporting consumables. Another, more sophisticated, approach that has been suggested[4] consists of developing a spectrum of

[4]See W. Walker et al., "From Components to Integrated Systems: Technological Diversity and Interactions Between Military and Civilian Sectors," in P. Gummett and J. Reppy (eds.), *The Relation Between Military and Civilian Technologies* (Dordrecht: Kluwer Academic Publishers, 1988), pp. 17–37, and S. Schofield, "Defense Technology, Industrial Structure and Arms Conversion," in R. Coopey et al. (eds.), *Defense Science and Technology: Adjusting to Change* (Reading: Harwood, 1993).

capabilities in which a country's manufacturing proficiency could be rated along a hierarchy of products ranging from complete systems at one end to low-level components at the other. At the higher end, the products concerned would be more clearly military, with decreasing differentiation between military and civilian products at the lower end. This approach can be schematically depicted in the following way:

Integrated weapon-information systems (ADGES)	Major weapons platforms (battleships)	Complete weapon-component parts (torpedoes)	Subsystems (gyroscopes)	Sub-assemblies (gun sights)	Components (integrated circuits)	Materials (semi-conductors)

While this schema represents simply one classification among many others, it illustrates the general point: creating an empirical map of a country's defense industrial base along this (or some other) line provides a means of assessing both the relative sophistication of its military supplies and the robustness of access enjoyed by its military forces to a range of defense products.

Warfighting Inventory and Support

The character of a country's military inventory and its combat support capabilities is the last, but obviously not the least, important category of military capability and effectiveness. In fact, collecting detailed information about the military inventories of other countries remains one of the staple pursuits of the intelligence community, and for good reason: when combined with the manpower component referred to earlier, a country's military inventory and its combat support assets constitute the usable "front-end" dimensions of force, force that can be used to defend one's own national interest as well as prevent others from reaching their own goals. The importance of such information has by no means diminished today. The intelligence community will continue to collect information pertaining to the number and kinds of tanks, guns, ships, airplanes, and other such instruments possessed by various countries. This information is generally easier to collect, since it consists of tangible components that can be seen and counted. But its utility ultimately derives from the fact that it pertains to the capacity for harm that one country can inflict on another. It also serves as a good substitute for estimating the extent of a state's commitment to its military when good information about defense budgets is unavailable. The investments made in such "bulk" military capabilities may in fact only grow with time, since it is quite possible that several countries not as sophisticated as the United States might respond to the incipient "revolution in military affairs" by simply increasing their numbers of combat systems—a solution that may be very consequential if the increases consist of modern, even if not revolutionary, warfighting components.

When the raw equipment possessed by countries is matched against the changing nature of warfare, the need for good data about some categories of inventory holdings and combat support—those relating to the ability to wage information-dominant war—has become more important than ever before. This does not imply that "bulk" military power appearing in the traditional forms of "dumb bombs and bullets" can be neglected, only that these forms have ceased to be instruments of high leverage. Thus, military holdings in various forms must continuously be monitored, but collection and assessment of such capabilities should be secondary to evaluating the presence and significance of more critical categories of equipment. These include the following:

- RSTA capabilities, which refer to reconnaissance, surveillance, and target acquisition technologies required for a "God's-eye view" at all levels—tactical, operational, and strategic—of the battlefield.
- Integrated battle management systems, which involve technologies that "net" together "sensors-to-shooters" in a seamless way.
- Precision strike weaponry, which refers to the congeries of guided and smart munitions that bequeath order-of-magnitude increases in accuracy, lethality, and effectiveness, again at all levels, tactical, operational, and strategic.
- Weapons of mass destruction, which refer to nuclear, biological, and chemical weapons that, together with their associated delivery and command-and-control systems, can cause high destruction and mass casualties among both military forces and civilian populations in relatively compressed timeframes.

- Agile, integrated, and protected logistics systems, which allow combat forces to sustain their military operations at high levels of intensity without either running out of crucial war materials or sustaining losses of such materials at possibly crucial moments of battle.

Each of these categories subsumes a large and diverse set of discrete technologies and organizational systems. Each, however, is critical for success on the modern battlefield, and the possession of such capabilities will enhance a military force's ability to prosecute a wide spectrum of operations. Consequently, collecting information about a country's holdings and capabilities in these areas will provide critical insight about its military's preparedness and ability to wage modern war.

CONVERSION CAPABILITY

While the availability of strategic resources is a critical ingredient of military capability, it is but part of the story. An effective military is one that can take these resources and "convert" them to create a modern force capable of conducting effective operations against a wide range of adversaries. This conversion process is critical because it determines whether the resources garnered from the country as a whole will finally produce a military force with operational competencies that make a strategic difference on the battlefield. Successfully converting available resources into effective military capability is therefore one real test of the quality of military leadership (success in battle is the obvious other key test), but as the discussion below will indicate, success in this arena may be dependent on structures and entities that go beyond the military itself.

Of the many factors that affect a military's ability to convert resources into operational capability, the following are the most important: (1) the threats facing a country, which change in a reactive fashion, and the strategy developed to cope with those threats; (2) the structure of civil-military relations, including the military's access to national leadership, which enables it to understand changing national goals, make its case for additional resources, and obtain the freedom to operate as required; (3) the density of foreign military-to-military relations, which determines access to other military forces and possible opportunities for learning, emulation, and analysis; (4) the nature of doctrine, training, and organization within a force, which functions as the glue that allows raw military resources to bind themselves into operationally effective social forms and combat practices; and (5) the potential and capacity for innovation, which determines whether a military force can cope with changing strategic and operational problems while continuously improvising solutions that keep it a step ahead of potential competitors. All these variables condition the ability of a military leadership to link the achievement of military effectiveness against its enemies with the resources it has available. Consequently, understanding how these qualitative factors affect military capability are important to the analysis of national power.

Threats and Strategy

As Williamson Murray and Mark Grimsley have noted, "the concept of 'strategy' is notoriously difficult to define."[5] At its broadest level, military strategy is the process by which a force matches its means (the resources provided to it) to its external problems. This process, being conditioned by developments occurring outside the military, in the final analysis involves "the rational and reciprocal adjustment of ends and means by rulers and states in conflict with their adversaries."[6] Strategy is what gives concreteness to the term "military power" insofar as it asks, and links, two crucial questions: What are the state's security objectives? What are the military capabilities needed to attain those objectives? Several specific external factors determine strategy. Fear, or its absence, importantly shapes strategy. States that believe they are insecure have a powerful incentive to develop an effective military strategy to protect themselves from those they perceive as threatening. The nature of a state's aims also affects its military strategy. A state with revisionist objectives must develop a strategy that is offensively oriented and maximizes its chances of prevailing over the adversary most likely to attempt frus-

---

[5]Williamson Murray and Mark Grimsley, "Introduction: On Strategy," in Williamson Murray, MacGregor Knox, and Alvin Bernstein (eds.), *The Making of Strategy: Rulers, States, and War* (Cambridge: Cambridge University Press, 1994), p. 1.

[6]MacGregor Knox, "Conclusion: Continuity and Revolution in the Making of Strategy," in Murray, Knox, and Bernstein, op. cit., p. 614.

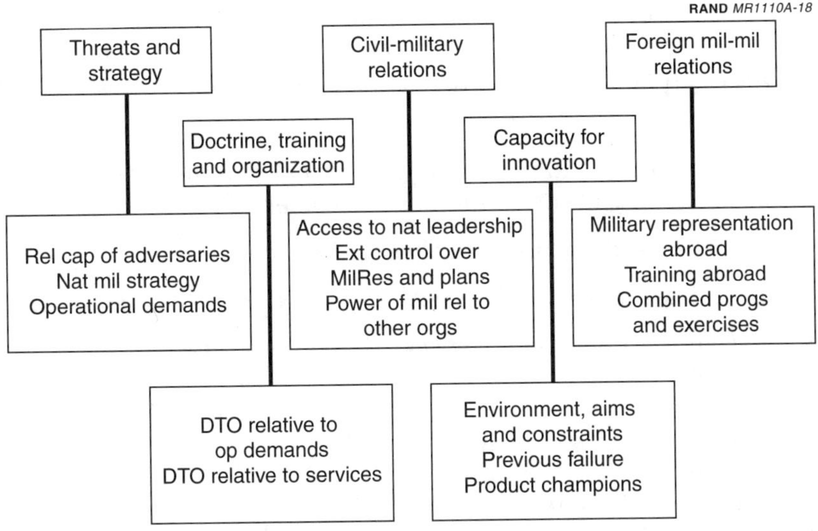

Figure 18—Components of Conversion Capability and Illustrative Indicators

trating the attainment of its aims. A state with extensive overseas interests must develop a deterrence-oriented strategy (to prevent challenges to those interests) and a power-projection strategy (to defend its overseas interests if deterrence fails).[7] Geography, of course, is also a very important factor affecting a state's military strategy.

Unlike orders of battle or weapons inventories, military strategy is impossible to quantify. But because a country's strategy is related so crucially to its military capability and effectiveness, understanding the nature of its strategy is vital because it identifies the kinds of military competencies that would have to be acquired and the ways in which military forces would generally be used. The generic signposts relating to these issues would be: the country's prior military strat-

---

[7]Barry Posen has pointed out that insular powers with important overseas interests invariably rely heavily on extended deterrence strategies. Barry Posen, *The Sources of Military Power: Britain, France, and Germany Between the World Wars* (Ithaca: Cornell University Press, 1984).

egy; existing doctrinal writings; extant equipment inventories; pattern of force deployments; and past training exercises.[8] When such information is integrated with geopolitical analysis assessing the country's

- geographic position, including critical geophysical features defining possible opportunities and vulnerabilities;
- most likely adversaries and allies in the event of conflict;
- historical roots, and continuity, of external policy and goals; and
- declaratory policy with respect to its strategic aims,

it is possible to discern whether a country's present military capability is adequate to the strategic tasks facing it and, if not, whether it is likely to respond by changing its present military size, structure, inventory, or warfighting strategy. To the degree that alterations in any of these arenas are seen to provide useful solutions to the outstanding political problems facing a country, it is likely that—*other things being equal*—its military leadership would gravitate toward, or argue for incorporating, such solutions. The threats facing a country and the strategy developed to cope with those threats thus become the first important conversion factor that allows resources to be transformed into effective warfighting competencies.

Structure of Civil-Military Relations

The structure of civil-military relations is another crucial variable that affects the conversion process, because the relationship between the holders of political and military power affects both the creation and the effective use of military forces. The problematic nature of civil-military relations is rooted in the fact that war often makes contradictory demands on the holders of political and military power. From the perspective of the latter, the extremity inherent in the application of military power is what makes it effective, and since success in the military realm often arises from the application of

---

[8]These generic signposts are adapted from Jeffrey A. Isaacson, Christopher Layne, and John Arquilla, *Predicting Military Innovation* (Santa Monica, CA: RAND, DB-242-A, 1999), p. 56.

decisive and overwhelming violence, military leaders generally feel compelled to design, procure, and employ force in a way that maximizes the prospects of victory on the battlefield. From the perspective of the former, however, military power is a lethal but volatile instrument whose successful use often depends on its susceptibility to control. Such control may have to be exercised at all levels: at the level of designing forces, to avoid giving needless offense to one's competitors; at the level of procurement, to avoid undercutting other critical social goals; and at the level of employment, to avoid strategies and tactics which however militarily effective may be counterproductive to the larger interests of the state. Because of this inherent tension between political objectives and the military means necessary to secure them, the nature of civil-military relations within a country becomes critical.

There are several models of civil-military relations. The most familiar are:

- The liberal model, characterized by integrated boundaries between the civil and the military, strong civilian control, and a military force oriented to coping with external threats;
- The authoritarian model, characterized by permeated boundaries between the civil and the military, strong civilian control, and a military oriented to coping with both external and internal threats; and
- The praetorian model, characterized by fragmented boundaries between the civil and the military, continual civil-military competition accompanied by occasional but tenuous civilian control, and a military oriented to coping with external threats and internal challenges to both the state and its own existence simultaneously.

Unfortunately, there is relatively little work to suggest which of these models might be better from the perspective of a country's ability to increase its military capability or effectiveness.[9] The utility of these models in the context of measuring national power, therefore,

---

[9]The best work to date on this question is Michael C. Desch, *Civilian Control of the Military: The Changing Security Environment* (Baltimore: The Johns Hopkins Press, 1999).

derives primarily from their being ideal flowcharts that help to identify various patterns of power and authority relations: irrespective of which model applies to a given country, intelligence analysts will still have to identify the personalities involved, the relative power of these individuals, and the general patterns of interaction between them, with an eye to uncovering answers to those critical issues identified earlier: What is the nature and level of access enjoyed by the military to the national leadership (if the two are in fact different)? What is the bureaucratic power of the military with respect to securing funding, controlling procurement, and directing its internal organization? What is the institutional structure that regulates the development of military strategy and tests its coherence with other national goals?

Foreign Military-to-Military Relations

In an era where knowledge is diffusing at a relatively rapid rate, the nature and extent of the relationships enjoyed by a country's military forces with their counterparts abroad can become an important ingredient that enables more effective conversion of national resources into usable military power. Military-to-military relations come in various forms. At the simplest level, the presence of defense attachés in embassies abroad functions as one conduit for monitoring new developments in technology, force structure, and organization. Participating in military education programs abroad and observing various foreign military exercises represents an interaction at a deeper, more significant level, especially if such participation is fairly continuous, is diverse with respect to the kind of instruction offered, and involves individuals who eventually return to postings in force training and combat development establishments back home. At the most sophisticated level, military-to-military relations take the form of combined exercises, combined training programs, and combined deployments for military missions. While there is no doubt a significant gradation even within this sophisticated level of interaction, military-to-military relations here offer the weaker participants an opportunity to deepen their problem-solving skills and to learn new techniques and concepts of operation. Ultimately, they are challenged to develop solutions relevant to their own situations, solutions which may incorporate alternatives devised by others.

Assessing the nature and extent of a military force's participation in such activities, then, becomes a useful indicator of a country's desire to increase its conversion efficiency. To the degree that a military force is given the opportunity and eagerly participates in such relationships, it can more effectively assess where it stands relative to other militaries while learning about new technologies, concepts of operations, and modes of employment. While learning is the most obvious effect of such encounters, it may not be the only one. In fact, a competent but relatively poorly endowed force may utilize its military-to-military experience to develop dissimilar solutions (or "asymmetric" responses) to common problems. The best test, therefore, of whether military-to-military relationships are having any effect on the conversion capability of a country's military would be to look for new developments in its force structure, doctrine, training, organization, or equipment that could be derived from its intercourse with other foreign military organizations.

Doctrine, Training, and Organization

Possessing resources in the form of raw equipment inventory and manpower is inadequate if these two assets are not appropriately structured and trained to solve certain operational tasks in a coherent way. Having sophisticated military technologies and a large mass of soldiers is one thing. Being able to use them effectively is something else. Today, more than ever before, the ability to *integrate* technology and manpower through doctrine, training, and organization becomes the crucial determinant of a military's ability to use its power effectively and thereby increase its battlefield capabilities.[10]

Doctrine is the first vital integrative threshold. Doctrine refers to the body of principles that specify how a military uses its assets on the battlefield. In effect, it details how the military plans to fight and as such provides the framework within which both technology and manpower interact to secure certain operational outcomes. Ineffective doctrine can negate all the advantages offered by superior

---

[10]See James F. Dunnigan, *Digital Soldiers: The Evolution of High-Tech Weaponry and Tomorrow's Brave New Battlefield* (New York: St. Martin's Press, 1996); Stephen Biddle, "Victory Misunderstood: What the Gulf War Tells Us About the Future of Conflict," *International Security*, Vol. 21, No. 2 (Fall 1996), pp. 139–179.

equipment and fighting men: as the history of armored warfare suggests, the doctrinal innovation of massing even modestly capable armored elements and using them as part of combined-arms teams made an operational difference that could not be emulated or countered even by technically superior armored forces when employed in "penny packets" and bereft of combined-arms support.[11]

Training represents a second key integrative threshold. Military forces that are inadequately trained will fail to make effective use of the equipment at their disposal, no matter how sophisticated it is: the Iraqi army in the Gulf War is a classic example of how a relatively modern military force can crumble under pressure if it cannot exploit the technology at its command because poor doctrine and even poorer preparation prevent effective use of its assets. In fact, the best evidence for the value of training derives from the experience of visiting units at U.S. training ranges like Fort Irwin and NAS Fallon, where the resident "OPFOR" and "Aggressor" units routinely humiliate often technically superior visiting formations during training exercises simply by virtue of their exceptional training, cohesion, doctrine, and preparation for "combat."

Organization is a third crucial integrative threshold because suboptimal command and coordinating structures can inhibit military effectiveness. For example, militaries with very rigid command structures, highly compartmented internal organizations, and/or officers chosen for political loyalty rather than operational competence are unlikely to display the initiative and flexibility needed to employ their weaponry with maximum effectiveness. The issue is not simply one of centralization versus decentralization: as several analyses have shown, information technology today can support either organizational form with equal felicity and probably with comparable effectiveness.[12] The crucial issue therefore may be one of "appropriateness": is the organizational structure of a force optimal for the missions it is tasked with executing? Other desiderata may include "adaptability," meaning the ability to shift from one

---

[11]The effects of superior doctrine in explaining the effectiveness of German armor have been detailed in James S. Corum, *The Roots of Blitzkrieg* (Lawrence: University Press of Kansas, 1992).

[12]See, for example, Robert R. Leonard, *The Art of Maneuver* (Novato: Presidio Press, 1991).

pattern of structuring to another as the situation demands, and "internal connectivity," meaning the degree of structural rigidities within a military force that keep the organization's information and resources from being appropriately disseminated.[13] Many nominally large military powers like China and India are much weaker than they appear at first sight simply because the organizational structures of their forces actually reduce the combat power they can bring to the battlefield. Even the United States is not immune to this problem, and many observers have argued, quite persuasively, that whatever its technological superiority, the U.S. military is unlikely to change its organizational structure sufficiently to truly revolutionize its combat power.[14]

In the final analysis, integration is more determinative of a military's capabilities than its inventory of equipment or its mass of manpower. Any military force can leap over the technological complexity thresholds that separate the various domains of warfare simply by acquiring the technologies in question. But surpassing the integrative thresholds to utilize these technologies effectively is much more difficult. For the intelligence community, evaluating the doctrine, training, and organization of a foreign military force therefore becomes all the more important if it is to reach credible assessments of a given military's conversion capabilities. Here too, a nested analysis becomes necessary. First, what is the country's military strategy? Second, what operational tasks are predicated by that strategy? Third, does the country possess the equipment and manpower to undertake those operational tasks? Fourth, is the doctrine, technol-

---

[13]In this connection, Glenn Buchan notes, for example, that "the U.S. track record in using satellites effectively to support military operations" is far from reassuring, "considering how long we have been in the satellite business." During the Gulf War, apparently "in some cases it worked very well, usually between organizations that dealt informally on the basis of handshakes and mutual support. In other cases, however, the 'ships passed in the night' and users who might have benefited from the information that space systems could have provided couldn't 'plug in' effectively. These problems have long been recognized, which makes the fact that they have not been solved adequately all the more frustrating." See Glenn C. Buchan, *One-And-A-Half Cheers for the Revolution in Military Affairs,* P-8015 (Santa Monica, CA: RAND, 1998), p. 19.

[14]See Richard Szafranski, "Peer Competitors, the RMA, and New Concepts: Some Questions," *Naval War College Review,* Vol. 49, No. 2 (1996), pp. 113–119.

ogy, and organization in each warfighting domain appropriate and adequate for the tasks sought to be attained?

Capacity for Innovation

The final dimension of conversion capability is a military force's potential and capacity for innovation. This variable generally determines whether a force can cope with the ever-changing strategic and operational problems facing it, while simultaneously being able to develop solutions to stay one step ahead of its potential adversaries. Innovation is a multidimensional phenomenon. At one level, it may refer to the ability to develop new warfighting concepts. At another level, it may refer to the ability to develop new integrative capacities: reorganized command structures, better doctrine and tactics, improved logistics, new training techniques, and the like. At a more trivial level, it may also refer to the ability to develop new technology or devise new technical solutions for an operational problem at hand. Irrespective of what kind of innovation is being discussed, the capacity of a given military force to be innovative is crucial to its ability to extract maximum mileage from its equipment and manpower. The analytical challenge from the perspective of measuring national power, then, consists of identifying those factors which might facilitate a high capacity for innovation within a given military force and, subsequently, translating these factors into indicators that could be tracked by the intelligence community.

From the extensive literature on military innovation, it is possible to identify three dominant perspectives that explain the possibility of military innovation: neorealist, societal, and organizational theory. Each offers distinctive, often competitive, views on what produces a capacity for military innovation.[15]

---

[15]There is also a fourth perspective on military innovation which could be called cultural theory, and it appears in the guise of theories of strategic and organizational culture. The cultural perspective is not discussed here, for several reasons. First, the concept of culture is amorphous and its use as an analytical category is controversial. Second, when the cultural perspective is used, each case becomes sui generis; the use of culture-based perspectives makes generalizations impossible. Third, the track record of culture-based analyses is generally weak from the perspective of producing systematic generalizations; other perspectives have far more explanatory power. With respect to the issue of military innovation, the strategic culture argument suffers from a very specific weakness: this perspective may tell the analyst something about a

The neorealist perspective on innovation is simple and straightforward: military forces having a high capacity to innovate are those which face a hostile security environment or are committed to supporting expansive foreign and strategic national policies. This perspective, in effect, identifies countries that have strong incentives to encourage their militaries to be innovative. Societal perspectives, in contrast, draw attention to internal factors that are necessary to facilitate innovation and in particular argue that the ability of military organizations to innovate is affected crucially by the relationship between the military and its host society.[16] In this view, the most effective and innovative militaries are those subsisting in a cohesive society. That a military is set in a divisive society does not necessarily mean that it will not or cannot innovate, but rather that this innovative capacity cannot be sustained over the long term. As Rosen argues:

> Military organizations that are separated from their host society and which draw on that society for resources are in tension with that society. They extract resources while being different from and under-representative of the larger society. This tension can and has created problems in prolonged war or prolonged peacetime competition. An innovative military that extracts resources but is isolated from society may not be able to sustain that innovation in periods of prolonged conflict.[17]

In contrast to the neorealist perspective, which identifies states that have incentives to innovate, and the societal perspective, which identifies states that have the kind of society-military relationships that can facilitate innovation, the organizational perspective identi-

---

state's grand strategic preferences, but it says nothing about the probability of whether the state will innovate militarily.

[16]See Stephen Peter Rosen, *Societies and Military Power: India and its Armies* (Ithaca: Cornell University Press, 1996), and Stephen Peter Rosen, "Military Effectiveness: Why Society Matters," *International Security,* Vol. 19, No. 4 (Spring 1995), pp. 5–31. A very useful discussion of the utility of societal perspectives—which often implicitly draw on notions of culture—can be found in Michael C. Desch, "Culture Clash: Assessing the Importance of Ideas in Security Studies," *International Security,* Vol. 23, No. 1 (Summer 1998), pp. 141–170.

[17]Stephen Peter Rosen, "Societies, Military Organizations, and the Revolution in Military Affairs: A Framework for Intelligence Collection and Analysis," unpublished manuscript, June 1996, p. 1.

fies states with particular organizational characteristics that can facilitate innovation. Although there are many approaches here, like the rational systems approach, the open systems approach, and the natural systems approach,[18] the last approach in organizational theory is the most appropriate framework for analyzing the capability of militaries to innovate, because organizations in real life act as less-than-rational systems thanks to cognitive constraints. The natural systems model is the dominant organizational theory paradigm. However, as applied to military innovation, this paradigm can be subdivided further into two different approaches: the "institutionalist" and "professionalist" schools.[19] Each of these has different implications with respect to military innovation.

The institutionalist approach holds that like all organizations, militaries are driven primarily by considerations of institutional well-being. As such, it is pessimistic about the likelihood that military organizations will innovate successfully.[20] This is because organizations are viewed as innately conservative. They are more concerned with the internal distribution of status and power than with organizational goals. In this milieu, new ideas are perceived as threatening.[21] Organizations are driven by the need to maintain organizational well-being (defined in terms of budget, manpower, and territory/domain) and to reduce uncertainty. Consequently, in organizations the focus is on short-term problem solving rather than long-term planning; standard operating procedures are used to maximize control over, and minimize uncertainty from, the external

---

[18]See, by way of example, W. R. Scott, *Organizations: Rational, Natural, and Open Systems* (New York: Prentice Hall, 3d ed., 1992); Graham Allison, *The Essence of Decision: Explaining the Cuban Missile Crisis* (Boston: Little, Brown, 1971); T. Farrell, "Figuring Out Fighting Organizations: The New Organizational Analysis in Strategic Studies," *The Journal of Strategic Studies* (March 1996); and James G. March and Herbert A. Simon, *Organizations* (New York: John Wiley & Sons, 1958).

[19]This typology is based on Emily O. Goldman, "Institutional Learning Under Uncertainty: Finds from the Experience of the U.S. Military," unpublished manuscript, Department of Political Science, University of California, Davis, 1996.

[20]Examples of this approach are Posen, *Sources of Military Doctrine,* and Jack Snyder, *The Ideology of the Offensive: Military Decisionmaking and the Disasters of 1914* (Ithaca: Cornell University Press, 1984).

[21]V. A. Thompson, *Bureaucracy and Innovation* (University, Alabama: University of Alabama Press, 1969), p. 22.

environment; and research is oriented to problem solving, undertaken to solve an immediate issue, not to innovate.[22] These impediments to innovation are likely to be overcome only when specific conditions are fulfilled. First, organizations that have recently experienced major failure are likely to be stimulated into innovation. Second, organizations with "slack" (that is, substantial uncommitted resources) are more likely to engage in innovation. Third, innovation will occur when the civilian leadership intervenes to force military organizations to innovate. This intervention is held to be necessary to overcome the status quo bias that is imputed to military organizations.

The professionalist approach, however, views militaries as organizations driven by the goal of maximizing their state's security.[23] The professionalist school is relatively optimistic about the likelihood that military organizations will innovate successfully, since it posits that under favorable conditions, organizations are capable of learning. In contrast to the institutionalist approach, the professionalist model assumes that military organizations undertake innovation on their own; that is, outside stimulus in the form of civilian intervention is not required to spur innovation. Military organizations will take the initiative to innovate because they are professional organizations driven by the goal of providing security for the state. The requisites for successful innovation are existence of senior officers with a new vision of future warfare ("product champions"); reform-minded junior officers; and the creation of new career paths within the organizations that allow the reform-minded younger officers to be promoted. Innovation is stimulated by competition and debate either within a branch of the military or between branches of the military.

From the perspective of assessing the prospects for innovation within a military force, these theoretical perspectives suggest that the

---

[22]Matthew Evangelista, *Innovation and the Arms Race: How the United States and the Soviet Union Develop New Military Technologies* (Ithaca: Cornell University Press, 1988), pp. 11–12; Posen, *Sources of Military Doctrine,* p. 54.

[23]See Stephen Peter Rosen, *Winning the Next War* (Ithaca: Cornell University Press, 1991).

intelligence community ought to be directing its gaze along the following lines.[24]

- Deriving from neorealist perspectives, the relevant questions are:
  - Does the country in question face a high threat environment?
  - Does the country in question seek to pursue revisionist aims?
  - Does the country in question face high resource constraints?
- Deriving from the societal perspective, the relevant question is:
  - Does the country in question exhibit high societal cohesion, and how is this cohesion (or lack thereof) reflected in the military?
- Deriving from the organizational perspective, the relevant questions are:
  - Has the country/military force in question experienced conspicuous failures in the past?
  - Are there identifiable "product champions" within the military?
  - Are there plausible paths for career enhancement as a result of resolving existing technological, organizational, or doctrinal problems facing the military?

Asked systematically, these questions provide a basis for anticipating military innovation. They cannot provide specific predictions about the particulars of any given innovation because the level of information about the problem to be resolved may never be available. However, these approaches provide a means of ordering the complexity of the problem in certain determinate and, hopefully, manageable ways.

The preceding discussion should suggest why conversion capability remains a critical dimension of a military's ability to transform its resources into warfighting competencies that are effective on the

[24]For a different approach to this question, see Thomas G. Mahnken, "Uncovering Foreign Military Innovation," *Journal of Strategic Studies*, Vol. 22, No. 4 (December 1999).

battlefield. But because these variables are for the most part qualitative, they are also difficult to track from the perspective of the intelligence community. They are nonetheless identified because their presence or absence makes a difference in the ability of a military force to attain the kinds of warfighting competencies identified in the next section. Reviewing a country's threats and the strategy developed to cope with those threats, the nature of its civil-military interaction, the level of emulation and/or counterresponses derived from its experiences with foreign militaries, and its own internal attempts at improving its doctrine, training, and organization as well as its capacity to innovate pays rich dividends, at any rate, because the ability to pose effective threats may often derive from the possession of high technology but certainly does *not* require the acquisition of such resources. Many countries, in fact, simply cannot afford to invest in either acquiring or mastering the use of leading-edge systems. Yet these countries can, in principle, be very consequential military threats. By coupling low technology with creative operational or tactical concepts, these countries can attain a high degree of military capability and may even be able to prevail against opponents employing superior military technology. This is a point that must not be lost sight of when "resource"-based conceptions of national power, like this one, are used for purposes of analysis.

At a time when U.S. military planners are increasingly concerned about "asymmetric strategies" or "asymmetric threats," this cautionary reminder becomes relevant *a fortiori*. As Bruce W. Bennett et al. have noted, "*asymmetric strategies are not so much about weapons as about the concepts of how war will be fought.*"[25] The bottom line for intelligence analysts thus is clear: without the context provided by a state's threat environment and its military strategy, conditioned further by how it handles other conversion factors relating to civil-military and foreign military relations, doctrine, training, and organization, and finally capacity for innovation, evaluating the capability or effectiveness of a country's military force is all but impossible.

---

[25]Bruce W. Bennett, Christopher P. Twomey, and Gregory F. Treverton, *Future Warfare Scenarios and Asymmetric Threats* (U) (Santa Monica, CA: RAND, MR-1025-OSD, 1999). Emphasis added.

COMBAT PROFICIENCY

When strategic resources are married to conversion capability, the result is a military force capable of undertaking a variety of combat operations against an adversary on the battlefield. The ability to undertake such combat operations remains the ultimate "output" of national power because it represents the means by which a country can secure its political objectives over and against the will of other competing entities if necessary. In a narrower sense, the ability to undertake combat operations also remains the ultimate "output" of the military establishment itself, because the latter too is created, sustained, and enlarged (if necessary) with the intent of being employed for the successful conduct of such operations.

Assessing the combat proficiency of a military force is by no means a simple matter. First, combat can occur in different, often multiple, realms simultaneously. Second, it involves numerous elements for success, elements which have been discretely identified earlier under the rubric of "strategic resources" and "conversion capability." Third, the balance of contending forces also matters significantly and in complex ways. Fortunately, the task here does not require assessing the combat proficiency of any given force, but rather simply explicating a methodology that identifies how such an assessment can be done in a way that accommodates a wide variety of military operations, ranging from simple to difficult, while simultaneously allowing for some meaningful comparisons among a small, select group of countries.

The methodology, described below, is drawn entirely from the pioneering work of Jeffrey A. Isaacson et al., undertaken at RAND in recent years. Although this research was conducted independently of the effort at measuring national power in the postindustrial age, Isaacson and his associates developed a framework for evaluating warfighting competencies that is simple (in an analytic sense) yet extremely fecund in that it accommodates the complexity of warfighting operations along a spectrum of competencies in three different dimensions of combat: ground, naval, and air operations. This "capability-based methodology" is not intended to predict combat outcomes, just as the framework for assessing national power described in this report is not intended to suggest that the countries judged more "powerful" in terms of its analysis will always prevail in interstate politics. Rather, it is meant to assess a country's present and potential ability to engage in an increasingly complex set of military operations, which may then be compared both across time and among a small group of comparably situated competitors. Given the systematic methodological affinity between Isaacson's approach to assessing warfighting competency and the framework for measuring national power offered in this report, it is easy to discern how the former becomes a fitting component of the latter's effort to integrate military capability as the most important ultimate manifestation of national power.

Isaacson's methodology, illustrated in Figure 19, is based upon the simple hypothesis that military capabilities (or warfighting competencies) may be arrayed along a spectrum of increasing complexity, with each realm of military operations—ground, naval, and air—having internal "domains" separated by "thresholds" of technology and integrative capacity.

Although Isaacson's analysis uses only "technology" and "integrative capacity" as the relevant variables, it is important to recognize that these are essentially *economizing abstractions* which include almost

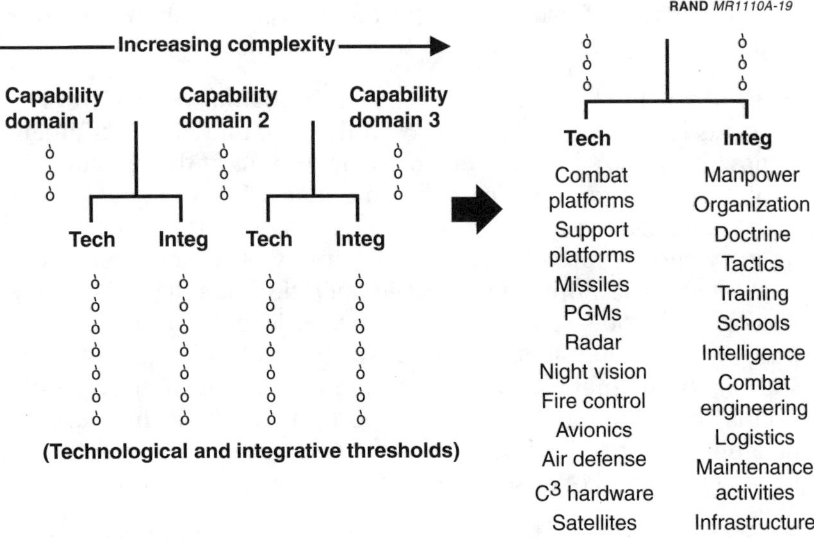

Figure 19—Understanding Military Competency

all the factors considered earlier under the rubric of "strategic resources" and "conversion capability." The methodology, therefore, suggests that increasing military capability (or extending one's warfighting competencies) requires a force to acquire not only new hardware, but actually develop the integrative dimensions that enable it to utilize its technology, manpower, and other supporting resources effectively. This simple idea is then applied to ground, naval, and air operations.

As Figure 20 shows, ground force competencies are arrayed along a spectrum ranging from irregular infantry operations at the simplest end to knowledge-based warfare at the complex end. *Irregular operations* consist mainly of ambushes, hit-and-run operations, and sniping activity, that can be prosecuted most efficiently in urban areas with limited equipment, mostly small arms, and small forces usually organized around the company level.

The next level of proficiency involves *coordinated infantry and artillery operations,* which impart the ability to mount static urban defense, including building robust fortifications backed up by artillery. Offensive capabilities at this level of proficiency usually are not manifested above battalion level and involve some vehicular assets, packets of armor, and portable ATGMs usually employed against vulnerable soft targets or fixed installations.

Elementary combined arms represents a qualitative leap from the previous levels of proficiency. With the capability for coordinated armor/mechanized mobile defensive operations at the brigade level, a military force can now carry out basic flanking and envelopment operations against attacking armor with mobile forces using both infantry and armored elements. The ability of these forces to conduct offensive armored/mechanized operations is still circumscribed and limited to heavily rehearsed, brigade-level attacks against exposed, vulnerable salients without subsequent exploitation or pursuit. Such capabilities, however, do allow for a deep attack capability against large, stationary targets like ports and airfields that may even be crudely coordinated with mobile defensive operations, and might include the use of offensive biological or chemical weapons.

Basic combined arms forces represent a greatly expanded version of the maneuver skills manifested at the previous level of competency.

Such forces can execute reasonably sophisticated division-level mobile defensive operations, featuring complete combined-arms operations: their defensive operations would include echeloned concentrations of armor, pinning attacks and feints, fire traps, and rapid shifts of forces from one sector to another, while their deep offensive operations, mostly restricted to the brigade level, could include armored attacks that employ creative turning movements and open the door to exploitation/pursuit operations. They can coordinate deep attacks with operations at the front and use special operations forces to target critical installations like radars, SAM sites, and communications bunkers with cruise and ballistic missiles.

Coordinated deep attack competencies differ from basic combined arms primarily with respect to the capacity to mount deep operations that emphasize rear echelon target kills. In particular, these forces can more accurately target corps-level rear echelon targets, such as assembly areas, truck parks, fuel dumps, and switching stations than can forces competent only in basic combined arms. In addition, these deep attacks can take place simultaneously with either offensive or defensive mobile operations at the front.

Full combined arms competencies represent an ability to conduct sophisticated mobile defensive operations at the corps level, including a mix of maneuver and firepower through the use of full combined-arms task forces. Turning, envelopment, flanking, and breakthrough operations can all be conducted with high skill by forces with such competencies. Defensive operations here can feature counterattacks of varying size as well as basic levels of joint operations, mainly air-ground cooperation in the form of integrated helicopter or fixed-wing close air support (CAS). Offensive operations would include potent division-level mobile capabilities that employ envelopment, turning, flanking, and bypassing operations, as well as full exploitation and pursuit. The ability to closely coordinate the deep and close battle in sequence implies that deep strikes with missiles and tactical aircraft against enemy rear echelons can be mounted just before or just after the critical close combat phase begins, and the acquisition of modest-quality night vision equipment heralds the prospect of round-the-clock operations.

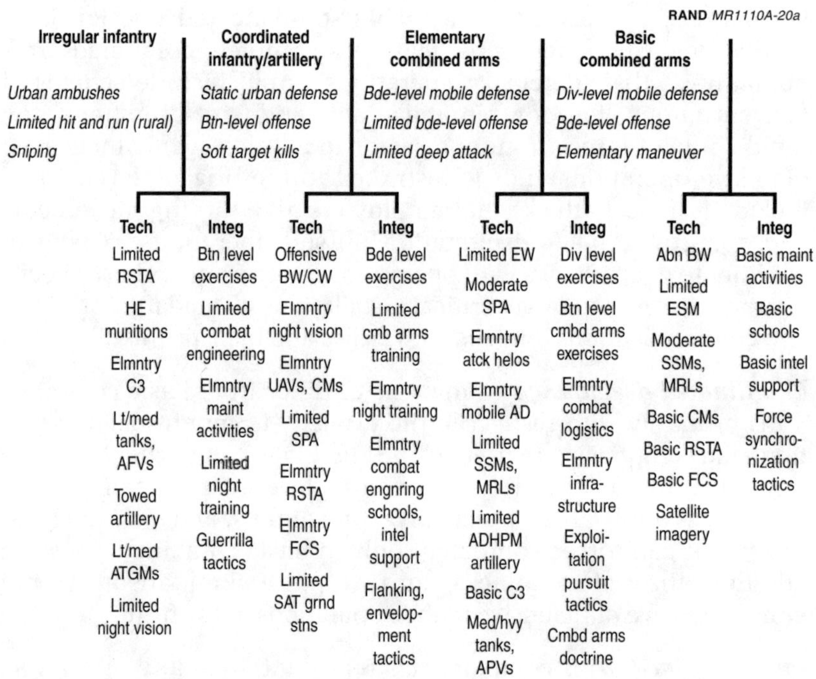

Figure 20—Assessing Ground Warfare Capabilities

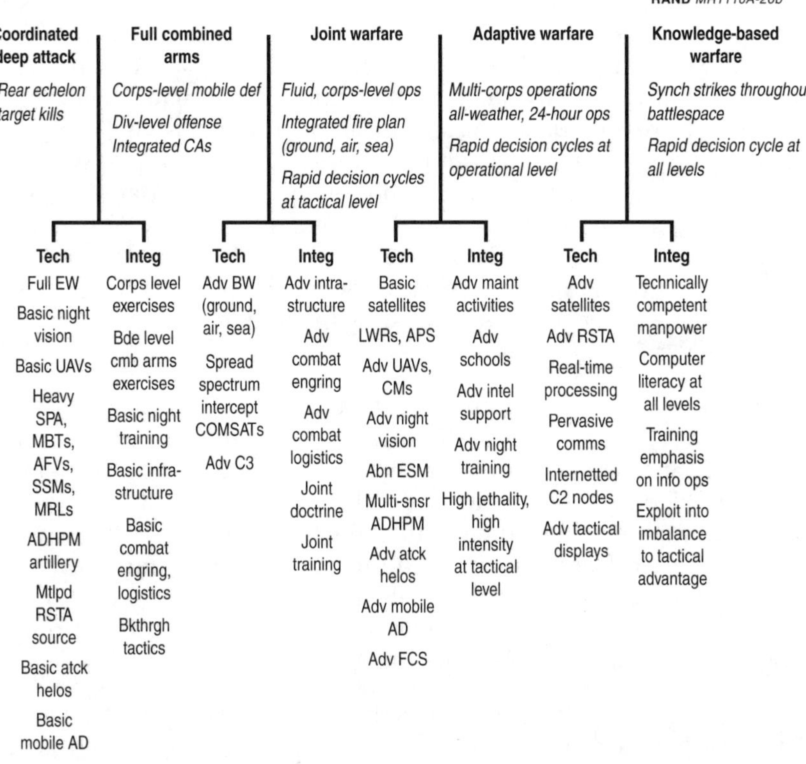

Figure 20—Assessing Ground Warfare Capabilities—extended

Joint warfare competency represents an entry into the realm of nonlinear warfare, wherein force-on-force annihilation no longer depicts the battle accurately. Forces capable of such operations can overwhelm an adversary by quickly paralyzing his command nodes with deep armored thrusts, missile attacks, and massive jamming/intercept operations, and can execute fluid armored operations at the corps level on both offense and defense. Such operations can potentially overload an opponent's command and control structure so heavily that systemic disorientation results in the inability to do anything more than simply react to the moves of the initiator. Joint warfare essentially consists of wresting the initiative from opponents through cognitive dominance at the tactical level.

Adaptive warfare competencies give a force the ability to conduct nonlinear operations at the multicorps level in both offense and defense. Such forces can launch deep attacks based on near-real-time intelligence data, operate at night and in adverse weather, and strike throughout the entire depth of the battlespace simultaneously. Under many circumstances, such forces can defeat more primitive opponents even when facing highly disadvantageous force-on-force ratios, and they can wrest the initiative from opponents through cognitive dominance at the operational level.

Knowledge-based warfare represents a competency that allows a force to achieve cognitive dominance over its opponents at all levels—strategic, operational, and tactical. Because such forces possess a near-perfect, dynamic picture of all unit positions in real time, these armies can get inside the adversary's decision cycle (the so-called "OODA loop") so rapidly that the latter's command structure will always be making decisions based on obsolete information. There is no army that has mastered knowledge-based warfare in existence today, but the U.S. Army's Force XXI vision represents a step toward this ideal.

The spectrum of naval force competencies has been structured in a manner analogous to that of ground forces (see Figure 21). *Coastal defense and mining* represent the most primitive naval warfighting competency in Isaacson's capabilities-based methodology. Such operations are the provenance of navies composed of small craft (under 70 feet), armed with small-caliber weapons, and used primarily to patrol coastal waters or lay mines for defensive operations.

Personnel engaged in such operations acquire ship-operating skills primarily from the fishing industry, and their limited weapons proficiency may require soldiers on board to handle weapons.

Coastal anti-surface warfare (ASuW) represents a marginal improvement in competency deriving from increased offensive capability, with converted Army weapons such as rocket-propelled grenades (RPGs), .50 caliber machine guns, and shoulder-launched rockets as the normal armament. In some cases, land-based missile batteries may be part of the weapons inventory. Forces at this level of competency typically operate ships as independent units, remain relatively close to shore, generally utilize line-of-sight (LOS) targeting of surface vessels, and possess limited VHF communications. For the most part, personnel acquire ship-handling skills from the commercial sector, but limited naval training may provide the skills required for weapons proficiency.

Anti-surface and anti-air warfare (AAW) with surface ships, including countermining and naval gun fire support (NGFS), represent further improvements in competency but nonetheless remain within the ambit of the simplest form of naval warfare: ship versus ship. Such forces are not capable of operating at large distances from the coast for extended periods, and ships generally sail independently. With increased experience and operating time at sea, several ships can perform as a small surface action group (SAG), with capabilities for limited air/surface search, LOS targeting of low-tech missiles, and naval gun fire support. The technology pertinent here includes corvettes, older frigates, destroyers, and minesweepers, but the larger size of these vessels and the more complicated weapon systems aboard them usually make for greater integrative demands. Ship-handling skills, more advanced than in the commercial sector, usually require formal training for their proper development (usually accomplished at a naval school or training base). In addition, damage control (DC), fire control (FC), and AAW create new training requirements. Finally, keeping large ships under sail—even to a limited degree—requires elementary logistics (e.g., supply) and maintenance activities (e.g., shipyards with skilled laborers).

Anti-surface warfare with submarines represents a higher level of competency relative to operations conducted with surface ships

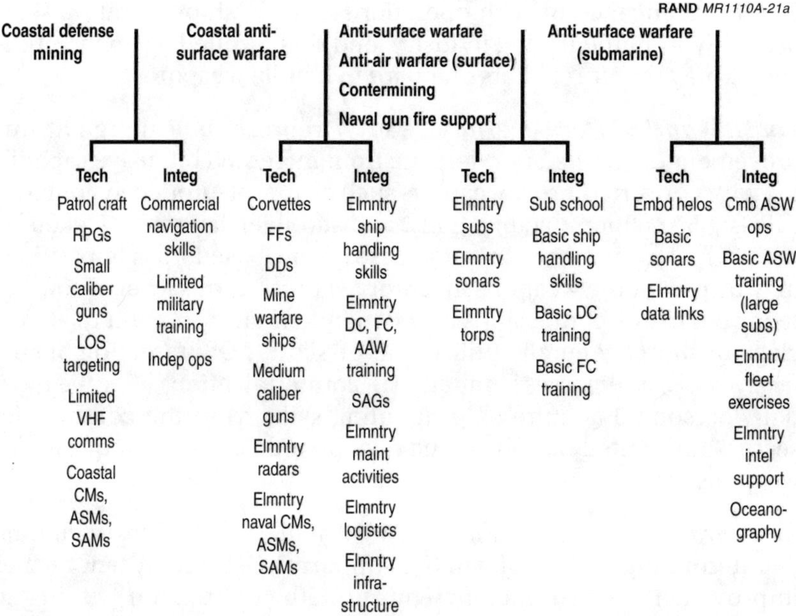

Figure 21—Assessing Naval Warfare Capabilities

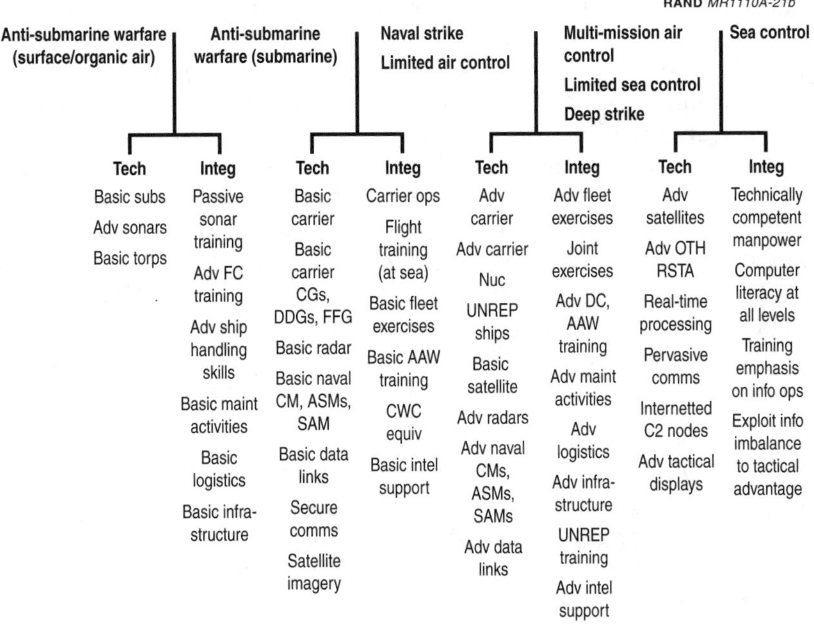

Figure 21—Assessing Naval Warfare Capabilities—extended

alone because of the complexity of submarine operations and the challenges of operating effectively under water. These operations usually take the form of small diesel submarines targeting military and civilian shipping traffic. Such vessels usually operate at moderate distances, and they require resupply and refueling, usually accomplished at a naval base. Typically, diesel submarines act independently and station themselves at geographic choke points. Although they involve high initial investment and operating costs, small diesel boats can provide a relatively potent stealth weapon under the right circumstances even if they are equipped with older-generation sonars and torpedoes. Training for submarine operations usually requires a dedicated submarine school, with a curriculum that includes improved weapons and sensor training to locate and destroy a target.

Anti-submarine warfare (ASW) with surface ships represents another step up in the spectrum of competency because it requires dedicated surface combatants with capable sonars, and usually an organic helicopter capability. Because ships and helicopters must now operate with each other to perform ASW, this competency imposes substantial demands on integration. Ship manning and aviation skills combine with greater maintenance requirements. Moreover, such operations require tactical coordination, including the capability to pass tactical information between units, either by voice or through tactical data links. Target submarines are also required for ASW training, so that elementary fleet exercises become important for realizing such competencies. In addition, sonar training, oceanography, and elementary intelligence support cannot be overlooked.

ASW with submarines represents a even higher level of competency in comparison to surface ASW because of technological requirements, relating to submarine quietness (through hull and propulsion design) and the possession of advanced passive sonar and fire control systems, as well as the high integrative demands owing to the inherent difficulty of subsurface ASW targeting. In this context, passive sonar operations and advanced fire control training are as important as the advanced ship-handling skills necessary to operate submarines effectively in an ASW environment. While nuclear submarines are excellent platforms for ASW, late-model diesels like the German Type 209 and Russian Type 636 Kilo can perform equally well in some missions. In any event, an advanced submarine fleet requires high levels of skilled maintenance and effective logistics support.

Naval strike and limited air control represents an important transition point in naval warfare competency because it signals the ability to project power ashore. Forces capable of such operations typically operate some type of aircraft carrier (perhaps a vertical/short takeoff and landing [V/STOL] carrier) with embarked aircraft capable of light attack. To support these operations, either satellite imagery or land-based long-range maritime patrol aircraft, together with intelligence support (for mission planning), are necessary for successful scouting and targeting. Because carrier operations are extremely demanding, an extremely high level of integrative efficiency is required. In addition to the carrier and its aircraft, the force structure required by this competency usually includes guided missile frigates, destroyers, and cruisers to protect the high-value assets against attack and to support the limited air control mission. These battlegroups usually perform basic fleet exercises, are capable of sharing moderate amounts of tactical data, and normally operate under some kind of component warfare commander (CWC) concept, whereby various commanders are assigned responsibility for defined mission areas so that coordinated defensive and offensive operations can be carried out simultaneously.

Multimission air control, limited sea control, and deep strike proficiencies come closest to realizing true "blue water" capability. Forces capable of such operations field advanced aircraft carriers capable of launching a variety of specialized conventional takeoff and landing (CTOL) aircraft, host advanced high-speed data transfer and communications systems, and possess sophisticated multidimensional offensive and defensive systems. Advanced cruise missiles with robust intelligence support provide a deep strike capability against both land and sea targets. In addition, under way replenishment makes forward presence possible, although a system of forward supply bases with ports can suffice in many instances. Such capabilities require advanced training and support, large-scale fleet exercises, and substantial joint operations. Moreover, an advanced shore establishment ensures that adequate maintenance and supply capabilities are available.

Comprehensive sea control is the naval equivalent of knowledge-based warfare in the realm of ground operations. In this case, over-the-horizon (OTH) reconnaissance, surveillance, and target acquisition (RSTA) systems, real-time processing, and pervasive communications create true network-centric forms of warfare that enable a force to successfully interdict an adversary's assets in any operating medium. Such capabilities promise an as-yet unseen multiplication of naval force effectiveness and remain an ideal that even the U.S. Navy can only aspire to today.

In a manner similar to the analysis of ground and naval warfare competencies, Isaacson develops an air warfare capabilities spectrum as well (see Figure 22). *Airspace sovereignty defense* remains the most primitive form of air warfare capabilities, and a force whose competencies are exhausted by this mission is usually equipped with lightly-armed air assets operating in tandem with ground-based radars. These forces can detect intrusions into their air space and defend it against unarmed adversaries. Little else is within the grasp of such a rudimentary force.

Elementary defensive counterair (DCA) represents an improved ability to defend one's air space against armed intrusion. While it may not suffice to conduct a sustained DCA campaign against a more advanced air force, it does allow for an ability to inflict some losses against a more advanced aggressor and to prevent a potential foe from conducting unlimited overhead reconnaissance. A force capable of such operations usually fields obsolete air defense fighters, which prosecute air-to-air engagements solely within visual range with cannon and early-generation missiles, and do not operate outside of fixed air defense corridors. Command and control procedures for such air forces are rigid and consist mainly of GCI operations, with pilot training being light and restricted to simple combat maneuvers.

Basic DCA and elementary strategic strike are in many ways similar to the previous level of competency except that such forces often field improved air defense fighters, improved AAMs and GCI radars, and operate out of hardened shelters that provide enhanced passive defense to the force as a whole. Pilot training also improves marginally to enable handling more sophisticated aircraft, but elementary logistics usually make for low operational tempos. In addition, using simple unmanned aerial vehicles (UAVs) or other forms of elementary aerial reconnaissance bequeath a nascent strategic strike capability, mostly useful for attacks against large, soft targets like cities and industrial plants.

Advanced DCA coupled with maritime defense (coastal) competencies represent a leap in capability over the previous level of proficiency. These forces possess some current-generation air defense aircraft armed with modern air-to-air missiles and possibly supported by airborne early warning (AEW) aircraft. They also exhibit an improved strike capability, utilize long-range, high-altitude aerial reconnaissance in the form of specially configured platforms, and possess the capability to deliver anti-ship missiles effectively within their coastal waters. Realizing such increased capabilities requires integrative investments, including advanced maintenance facilities, dedicated support, relatively high levels of training, and sophisticated command, control, and communications (C^3). The importance of integrative factors sharply increases in this domain, and air forces focusing on technological improvements alone are not likely to realize the full capabilities possible in this regime.

Battlefield air interdiction (BAI), basic strategic strike, and maritime strike competencies enable a force to influence ground combat in a manner impossible for forces with lower levels of capability. Utilizing basic attack aircraft, ground surveillance radars, cluster munitions, and basic anti-armor PGMs, such forces can influence the tactical battlefield while also reaching out to targets in the strategic realm. Here, such forces usually rely on their own air-breathing reconnaissance platforms or on foreign-supplied satellite data for targeting; they may also possess aerial refueling technology and air-launched cruise missiles (ALCMs) to strike an array of deep (i.e., greater than 300 km) targets like large surface-to-air missile (SAM) sites or surface vessels operating outside of their coastal waters. Pilot training in such forces is usually extensive, and a well-organized logistics system is usually available for combat support.

Fixed-wing close air support, basic suppression of enemy air defenses (SEAD), and basic deep interdiction remain competencies associated with highly advanced and capable regional air forces. Such forces utilize real-time communications with mobile ground units and can provide direct air support to ground elements engaged in close com-

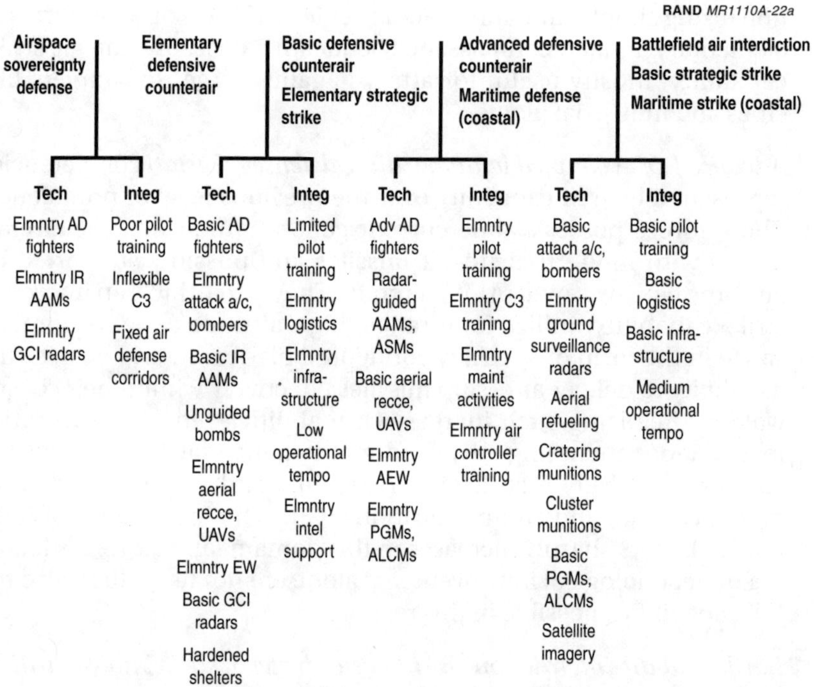

Figure 22—Assessing Air Warfare Capabilities

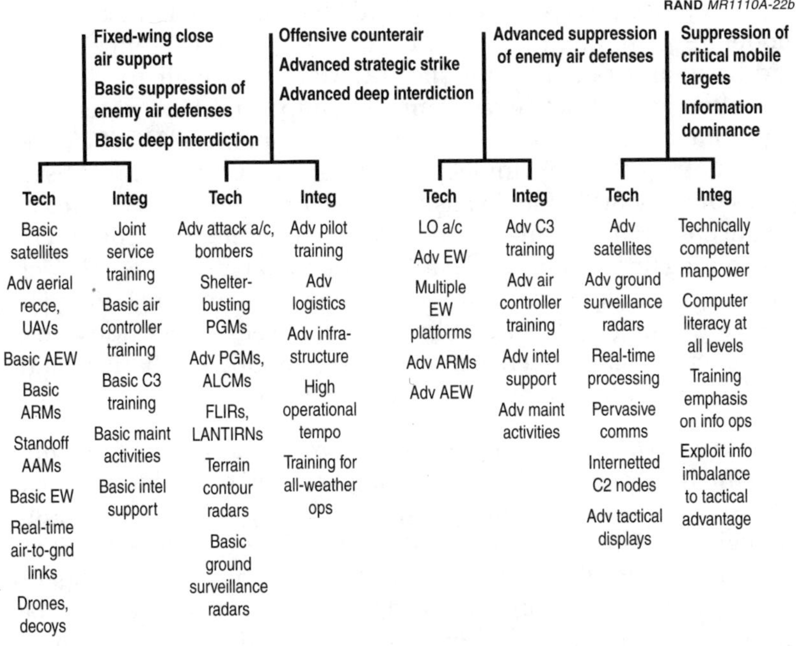

Figure 22—Assessing Air Warfare Capabilities—extended

bat. They also possess an established SEAD capability that includes moderate jamming, the use of decoy and reconnaissance drones, and basic anti-radiation missiles (ARMs). In the air-to-air realm, they often possess active radar missiles, improved AEW systems, and highly integrated air defense ground environments (ADGES), potentially making them formidable air-to-air adversaries for most air forces of the world. Finally, using small, independent satellites and advanced aerial reconnaissance they can execute deep interdiction missions against mobile and hard stationary targets. Creating such a force involves significant integration requirements, including joint service training with an emphasis on C^3, well-trained forward air controllers (FACs), effective intelligence support, and basic facilities and manpower for maintaining advanced systems.

Offensive counterair (OCA), advanced strategic strike, and advanced deep interdiction capabilities allow an air force to conduct a decisive offensive counterair campaign that includes airbase suppression through a day/night/all-weather deep interdiction campaign. Such a force possesses advanced attack aircraft, sophisticated navigation and targeting sensors, and highly capable ground surveillance radars. Its weapons include shelter-busting munitions, advanced air-launched cruise missiles utilizing GPS guidance, and advanced precision-guided munitions that can be used in high-intensity operations conducted at high tempos. Thanks to intensive and sophisticated training regimes, advanced logistics, and sizable ordnance stockpile, this type of air force can seal off the ground battlefield from enemy reinforcements for substantial portions of time.

Advanced SEAD competencies allow a force to rapidly paralyze even the most advanced air defense systems. Using low observable (LO) aircraft and munitions, sophisticated jamming from multiple platforms, spoofing, intelligent anti-radiation missiles, and advanced AEW, this force can achieve theater-level air supremacy more rapidly and at less cost than a force at the previous level of competency. This force invests heavily in C^3 training, air controller training, intelligence support, and maintenance activities to allow for high levels of sortie generation and effectiveness that are "second to none." The U.S. Air Force is the sole exemplar of this level of air power competency.

Suppression of critical mobile targets (CMTs) and information dominance represents a capability whereby a force relies on information imbalances to paralyze its adversaries and dominate its battlespace. Using real-time data processing and pervasive communications, it can destroy critical mobile targets (e.g., mobile missile launchers, mobile command posts) with a high level of confidence. This force can typically sustain a fleet of advanced ground surveillance aircraft in theater, a robust theater missile defense (TMD) capability, and a fully rounded out indigenous satellite capability that produces photo, infrared, and radar imagery in real time. Its tracking radars and air-based targeting sensors are more advanced than any fielded currently, and its well-trained, technically competent manpower can fully exploit them to perform CMT spotting and attacking adversaries effectively even in forested or mountainous terrain. This type of force remains an ideal for now.

The purpose of such a methodology is to locate the military competencies of a country on a schematic map that allows the analyst to depict its relative capabilities. The advantage of Isaacson's framework is that it allows military capabilities to be perceived not simply in terms of what countries possess but rather in terms of what can be achieved—with respect to operational competency—as a consequence of their possessions. It allows for the integration of both their strategic resources and their conversion capabilities, but ultimately it assesses their military power in terms of operational proficiencies that can be attained as a result of these interacting variables. The methodology can thus be used both in a static and in a comparative-static sense. It can locate the military capabilities of a country at a given point in time and in fact compare those capabilities to a select group over peers. If the relevant data are collected continuously, however—as the U.S. government invariably does—they can be used to measure progress diachronically both with respect to how a given country has improved (if it has) relative to its own past performance and with respect to other competitors or rivals that may be arrayed against it. In that sense, Isaacson's methodology allows for both absolute and relative comparisons of military competency across time. Clearly, the methodology itself is by no means sacrosanct. It is possible to devise other, or perhaps even better, methodologies. What is most important, however, is that it provides a structured way of combining data that are openly available—for example, about inventories—with data that are classified—for example, about logistics and training practices—to arrive at a more sophisticated, evaluative assessment of a country's military capability, which, as argued earlier, remains the final manifestation of national power.

Chapter Eight

CONCLUSION

This report has attempted to offer a comprehensive framework for evaluating the national power of countries in the postindustrial age. By its very nature, it is fairly detailed in structure and incorporates a variety of traditional and nontraditional indicators that bear on the production of national power today. This complexity is unavoidable, since the intent is to provide a framework for evaluating the national power of a few candidate great powers that are judged to be significant for future international politics. This framework must therefore be viewed as a complement to the single-variable measures of national power previously offered by many political scientists. These simple measures perform a useful sorting function in that they provide a means of identifying which countries are likely to be most relevant from the perspective of global power politics. But their very parsimony, which is so valuable for the purpose of rank ordering the many entities populating the international system, becomes a sharp limitation when detailed evaluations of a few, relevant countries are required.

The framework offered in this report is an effort to provide a template that allows a focused scrutiny of the national power profile of a single country (or of a few countries, one at a time). Toward that end, it has sought to capture multiple dimensions of power: (1) national resources, required to generate effective power today; (2) national performance, which derives from external pressures, the character of state-society relations, and the ideational clarity of both state and societal agents, and determines a state's ability to develop the resources necessary to dominate both the cycles of innovation and the creation of hegemonic potential; and (3) military capability, which constitutes the sword a polity brings to bear in international politics, manifested in the form of strategic resources, conversion capability, and warfighting competencies.

Admittedly, such an analytical framework privileges the state as the unit of analysis in international politics. It does not examine the extent to which the state may be either in retreat or growing in power as a result of developments in the substatal and transstatal realms. Incorporating variables from these levels of analysis remains work for future research. In any event, the present framework is offered as a first cut in search of further improvement. These improvements, ideally, can be incorporated at two levels: first, it is possible to propose a better framework than the one suggested here for purposes of creating a "national power profile" on key countries in the international system; second, even if the present framework is acceptable (with or without modifications), it is possible to propose better measures for many of the variables now incorporated. Finally, it would be useful to test this framework by using it to organize data collection for one or two countries on an experimental basis. This work, which is currently under way at RAND, will enable further refinement and improvement of the framework itself.

If such a framework is useful—after all the requisite improvements are incorporated—it could become the basis for assessing changes in national capability over extended periods of time. With a few modifications, it would also be useful when applied in a retrospective mode to assess the national capabilities of great powers in the past. Used in either way, it would improve our understanding of what makes nations powerful in international politics.

Appendix

QUANTITATIVE INDICATORS OF NATIONAL POWER

The following short list of indicators illustrates the *minimally necessary quantitative* information for judging national capabilities in the postindustrial age. Not all information pertaining to qualitative variables like the political environment in or outside the country, the nature of national political aims, the relationship between state, elites and masses, or the nature of military strategy—while important for evaluative assessments—is included in the list.

NATIONAL RESOURCES

Technology

Information and communications

Materials

Manufacturing

Biotechnology and life sciences

Aeronautics and surface transportation

Energy and environment

Militarily critical technologies

- Existing production capabilities
- Public and private R&D expenditures in critical civilian and military technologies

Enterprise

Capacity for invention

- Gross public and private expenditure in R&D
- Gross public and private expenditure in R&D/GNP
- Level of domestic/U.S. patenting in critical technologies

Capacity for innovation

- Number of patents adopted for manufacture

Diffusion of innovation

- Level of nationwide IT connectivity
- Number of trade/industry research organizations

Human Resources

Formal education

- Gross public and private expenditure on education
- Gross public and private expenditure on education/GNP and gross public and private expenditure on education per capita
- Gross public and private expenditure on education by level: primary; secondary; tertiary; vocational; continuing
- Enrollment and attainment rates by level (including foreign enrollment)
- Composition of specialization at secondary and tertiary and by category: math and physical sciences-biological sciences-engineering-social sciences and behavioral sciences-arts and humanities
- Number of specialized research institutes (especially in critical technology areas)

Financial/capital resources

Extent of savings

- Level of public and private saving/GNP
- Level of foreign direct and portfolio investment

Aggregate growth

- Size and growth rate of GNP and size and growth rate of GNP per capita

Sectoral growth

- Relative sector outputs and growth rates of different sectors (especially manufacturing and "knowledge production" sectors)

Physical resources

Energy

Critical minerals

- Level of domestic production and extent of foreign access

NATIONAL PERFORMANCE

Infrastructural capacity

Ratio of direct and indirect/international trade taxes

Ratio of nontax revenue/direct taxes

Actual tax revenue/taxable capacity measured relative to comparable peers

Ideational resources

National performance in TIMSS tests

Levels of public finance support for R&D and investment in critical technologies

Levels of public finance support for investment in human capital formation

MILITARY CAPABILITY

Strategic resources

Absolute size of defense budget

Size of defense budget relative to GNP and comparable peers

Education attainment levels of enlisted and officer corps

Number of combat RDT&E institutions

Number of advanced training facilities

Holdings of high-leverage combat systems

Conversion capability

Extent of military training abroad

Number of high-level joint military exercises

Combat proficiency

Various technology and integration indicators

BIBLIOGRAPHY

Alchian, Armen A., "Uncertainty, Evolution, and Economic Theory," *Journal of Political Economy,* Vol. 58, No. 3, June 1950.

Alcock, Norman Z., and Alan G. Newcombe, "The Perception of National Power," *Journal of Conflict Resolution,* Vol. 14, 1970.

Aldrich, Howard E., *Organizations and Environments,* Englewood Cliffs, NJ: Prentice-Hall, 1979.

Allison, Graham, *The Essence of Decision: Explaining the Cuban Missile Crisis,* Boston: Little, Brown, 1971.

Arendt, Hannah, *The Human Condition,* Chicago: University of Chicago Press, 1958.

Arquilla, John, "The Strategic Implications of Information Dominance," *Strategic Review,* Summer 1994.

Baldwin, David A., "Power Analysis and World Politics: New Trends Versus Old Tendencies," *World Politics,* Vol. 31, No. 2, January 1979.

Bankes, Steve, and Carl Builder, *Seizing the Moment: Harnessing the Information Technologies,* Santa Monica, CA: RAND, N-3336-RC, 1992.

Barnett, Correlli, *The Pride and the Fall: The Dream and Illusion of Britain as a Great Nation,* New York: Free Press, 1986.

Bean, Richard, "War and the Birth of the Nation State," *Journal of Economic History,* Vol. 33, 1977.

Bell, Daniel, *The Coming of Post Industrial Society: A Venture in Social Forecasting,* New York: Basic Books, 1973.

Bendix, Reinhard, *Kings or People: Power and the Mandate to Rule,* Berkeley: University of California Press, 1978.

Bennett, Bruce W., Christopher P. Twomey, and Gregory F. Treverton, *Future Warfare Scenarios and Asymmetric Threats* (U), Santa Monica, CA: RAND, MR-1025-OSD, 1999.

Biddle, Stephen D., "The European Conventional Balance: A Reinterpretation of the Debate," *Survival.*

———, "Victory Misunderstood: What the Gulf War Tells Us About the Future of Conflict," *International Security,* Vol. 21, No. 2, Fall 1996.

Bimber, Bruce A., and Steven W. Popper, *What Is a Critical Technology?* Santa Monica, CA: RAND, DRU-605-CTI, 1994.

Blaug, Mark, *The Cambridge Revolution: Success or Failure?* London: Institute of Economic Affairs, 1974.

Boudon, Raymond, and Francois Bourricaud, *A Critical Dictionary of Sociology,* Chicago: University of Chicago Press, 1989.

Bousquet, Nicole, "From Hegemony to Competition: Cycles of the Core?" in Terence K. Hopkins and Immanuel Wallerstein (eds.), *Processes of the World-System*, Beverly Hills: Sage, 1980.

Bracken, Paul, "The Military After Next," *The Washington Quarterly,* Vol. 16, No. 4, Autumn 1993.

Bremer, Stuart A., "National Capabilities and War Pronenes," in J. David Singer (ed.), *The Correlates of War II: Testing Some* Realpolitik *Models,* New York: Free Press, 1980.

Buchan, Glenn C., *One-And-A-Half Cheers for the Revolution in Military Affairs,* Santa Monica, CA: RAND, P-8015, 1998.

Burt, R. S., "Power in a Social Topology," in R. J. Liebert and A. W. Imershein (eds.), *Power, Paradigms, and Community Research,* Beverly Hills: Sage, 1977.

Cairncross, A. K., "The Place of Capital in Economic Progress," in L. H. Dupriez (ed.), *Economic Progress,* Louvain: International Economic Association, 1955.

Calder, Kent E., *Pacific Defense,* Princeton: Princeton University Press, 1996.

Champernowne, D. G. "The Production Function and the Theory of Capital: A Comment," *Review of Economic Studies,* Vol. 21, 1954.

Claude, Inis L., *Power and International Relations,* New York: Random House, 1962.

Cohen, Eliot, "A Revolution in Warfare," *Foreign Affairs,* Vol. 75, No. 2, 1996.

Cooper, Jeffery R., *Applying Information Technologies to Low-Intensity Conflicts: A Real-Time Information Shield Concept,* Arlington: SRS Technologies, 1992.

Corum, James S., *The Roots of Blitzkrieg,* Lawrence: University Press of Kansas, 1992.

Dahl, Robert, "The Concept of Power," *Behavioral Science,* Vol. 2, July 1957.

———, "Power," in the *International Encyclopaedia of the Social Sciences,* Vol. XII, New York: Free Press, 1968.

Davis, Kingley, "The Demographic Foundations of National Power," in Morrow Berger et al. (eds.), *Freedom and Control in Modern Society,* New York: Farrar, Straus & Giroux, 1954.

Denison, E., *The Sources of Economic Growth in the United States and the Alternatives Before Us,* New York: Committee for Economic Development, 1962.

Desch, Michael C., *Civilian Control of the Military: The Changing Security Environment,* Baltimore: The Johns Hopkins Press, 1999.

———, "Culture Clash: Assessing the Importance of Ideas in Security Studies," *International Security,* Vol. 23, No. 1, Summer 1998.

Deutsch, Karl W., *The Analysis of International Relations,* Englewood Cliffs: Prentice-Hall, 1968.

Di Maggio, Paul J., and Walter K. Powell, "The Iron Cage Revisited: Institutional Isomorphism and Collective Rationality in Organizational Fields," *American Political Science Review,* Vol. 48, April 1983.

Dietz, Mary, "The Slow Boring of Hard Boards: Methodical Thinking and the Work of Politics," *American Political Science Review,* Vol. 88, No. 4, December 1994.

Dunnigan, James F., *Digital Soldiers: The Evolution of High-Tech Weaponry and Tomorrow's Brave New Battlefield,* New York: St. Martin's Press, 1996.

Echevarria, Antulio J., and John M. Shaw, "The New Military Revolution: Post Industrial Change," *Parameters,* Winter 1992–93.

Evangelista, Matthew, *Innovation and the Arms Race: How the United States and the Soviet Union Develop New Military Technologies,* Ithaca: Cornell University Press, 1988.

Farrell, T., "Figuring Out Fighting Organizations: The New Organizational Analysis in Strategic Studies," *Journal of Strategic Studies,* March 1996.

Ferris, W., *The Power Capabilities of Nation-States,* Lexington: Lexington, 1973.

Freeman, C., *The Economics of Industrial Innovation,* Cambridge: MIT Press, 1982.

Friedberg, Aaron, "Why Didn't the United States Become a Garrison State?" *International Security,* Vol. 16, Spring 1992.

Fucks, Wilhelm, "Formeln zur Macht: Prognosen uber Volker," *Wirtschaft Potentiale,* Verlags-Anstalt, 1965.

German, F. Clifford, "A Tentative Evaluation of World Power," *Journal of Conflict Resolution,* Vol. 4, 1960.

Giddens, Anthony, *The Nation-State and Violence,* Berkeley: University of California Press, 1985.

Gilbert, Felix, "From Clausewitz to Delbruck and Hintze," *Journal of Strategic Studies,* Vol. 3, 1980.

Gilpin, Robert, *The Political Economy of International Relations,* Princeton: Princeton University Press, 1987.

———, *War and Change in World Politics.* Cambridge: Cambridge University Press, 1981.

Goertz, Gary, and Paul F. Diehl, *Territorial Changes and International Conflict,* London: Routledge, 1992.

Goldberger, Marvin L., Brendan A. Mahler, and Pamela Ebert Flattau (eds.), *Research-Doctorate Programs in the United States,* Washington, D.C.: National Academy Press, 1995.

Goldfinger, Charles, *The Intangible Economy and Its Implications for Statistics and Statisticians,* paper presented at the Eurostat-ISTAT seminar, Bologna, February 1996.

Goldman, Emily O., "Institutional Learning Under Uncertainty: Finds from the Experience of the U.S. Military," unpublished manuscript, Department of Political Science, University of California, Davis, 1996.

Goldstein, Joshua S., *Long Cycles: Prosperity and War in the Modern Age,* New Haven: Yale University Press, 1988.

Goure, Dan, "Is There a Military-Technical Revolution in America's Future?" *The Washington Quarterly,* Vol. 16, No. 4, 1993.

Gramsci, Antonio (ed. and intro. by Joseph A. Buttigieg; trans. Joseph A. Buttigieg and Antonio Callari), *Prison Notebooks,* vols. 1 and 2, New York: Columbia University Press, 1992, 1996.

Granbard, A. "Notes Toward a New History," in J. Cole, E. Barber, and A. Granbard (eds.), *The Research University in a Time of Discontent,* Baltimore: Johns Hopkins, 1994.

Griliches, Z., "Patent Statistics as Economic Indicators: A Survey," *Journal of Economic Literature,* Vol. 28, December.

Hall, John A. and John Ikenberry, *The State,* Minneapolis: University of Minnesota Press, 1989.

Hall, Peter G. and Paschal Preston, *The Carrier Wave,* Boston: Unwin & Hyman, 1988.

Hammond, Paul Y., "The Political Order and the Burden of External Relations," *World Politics,* Vol. 19, 1967.

Hannan, Michael T. and John Freeman, "The Population Ecology of Organizations," *American Journal of Sociology,* Vol. 82, No. 5, 1977.

Hart, Jeffery, "Three Approaches to the Measurement of Power in International Relations," *International Organization,* Vol. 30, 1976.

Hawley, Amos, "Human Ecology," in D. Sills, (ed.), *International Encyclopedia of the Social Sciences,* Princeton: Princeton University Press, 1968.

Hennings, K. H., "Capital as a Factor of Production," in John Eatwell, Murray Milgate, and Peter Newman (eds.), *Capital Theory: The New Palgrave,* New York: W. W. Norton, 1990.

Herrera, Amilcar, "Social Determinants of Science Policy in Latin America: Explicit Science Policy and Implicit Science Policy," in Charles Cooper (ed.), *Science, Technology and Development,* London: Frank Cass, 1973.

Hicks, John R., "Capital Controversies, Ancient and Modern," in John R. Hicks, *Economic Perspectives,* Oxford: Clarendon Press, 1977.

Hintze, Otto, "Military Organization and the Organization of the State," in Felix Gilbert (ed.), *The Historical Essays of Otto Hintze,* Princeton: Princeton University Press, 1975.

Hitch, Charles, and Roland McKean, *The Economics of Defense in the Nuclear Age,* Cambridge: Harvard University Press, 1960.

Hobbes, Thomas, *The Elements of Law,* Bristol: Thoemmes Press, 1994.

Holsti, Kal J., *International Politics: A Framework for Analysis,* Englewood Cliffs: Prentice-Hall, 1983.

Hufbauer, Gary, *Synthetic Materials and the Theory of International Trade,* London: Duckworth, 1966.

Isaacson, Jeffrey A., Christopher Layne, and John Arquilla, *Predicting Military Innovation,* Santa Monica, CA: RAND, DB-242-A, 1997.

Ishikawa, Shigeru, "A Note on the Choice of Technology in China," in Charles Cooper (ed.), *Science, Technology and Development,* Frank Cass: London, 1973.

Jaggers, Keith, "War and the Three Faces of Power: War Making and State Making in Europe and America," *Comparative Political Studies,* Vol. 25, No. 1, April 1992.

Jewkes, J., D. Sawers, and R. Stillerman, *The Sources of Invention,* London: Macmillan, 1958.

Jones, Lyle V., Gardner Lindzey, and Porter E. Coggeshall (eds.), *An Assessment of Research-Doctorate Programs in the United States: Mathematical and Physical Sciences,* Washington, D.C.: National Academy Press, 1982.

Katzenstein, Peter J., "Conclusion: Domestic Structures and Strategies of Economic Policy," *International Organization,* Vol. 31, Autumn 1977.

Kennedy, Paul, *The Rise and Fall of the Great Powers,* New York, Random House, 1987.

Kessel, Kenneth A., *Strategic Minerals: U.S. Alternatives,* Washington, D.C.: National Defense University Press, 1990.

Khalilzad, Zalmay M., and John White (eds.), *The Changing Role of Information in Warfare,* Santa Monica, CA: RAND, 1999.

Knight, F. "Diminishing Returns from Investment," *Journal of Political Economy,* Vol. 52, March 1944.

Knorr, Klaus, *Power and Wealth,* New York: Basic Books, 1973.

———, *The War Potential of Nations,* Princeton: Princeton University Press, 1956.

Knox, MacGregor, "Conclusion: Continuity and Revolution in the Making of Strategy," in Williamson Murray, MacGregor Knox, and Alvin Bernstein (eds.), *The Making of Strategy: Rulers, States, and War,* Cambridge: Cambridge University Press, 1994.

Krasner, Stephen D., *Defending the National Interest,* Princeton: Princeton University Press, 1978.

Kugler, Jacek, and Marina Arbetman, "Choosing Among Measures of Power: A Review of the Empirical Record," in Richard J. Stoll and Michael D. Ward (eds.), *Power in World Politics,* Boulder: Lynne Rienner, 1989.

Kugler, Jacek, and William Domke, "Comparing the Strength of Nations," *Comparative Political Studies,* Vol. 19, No. 1, April 1986.

Kuznets, Simon S., "Schumpeter's Business Cycles," *American Economic Review,* Vol. 30, No. 2, 1940.

Lamborn, Alan C., "Power and the Politics of Extraction," *International Studies Quarterly,* Vol. 27, 1983.

Lasswell, Harold D., and Abraham Kaplan, *Power and Society,* New Haven: Yale University Press, 1950.

Layne, Christopher, "The Unipolar Illusion: Why New Great Powers Will Rise," *International Security,* Vol. 17, No. 4, Spring 1993.

Leonard, Robert R., *The Art of Maneuver,* Novato: Presidio Press, 1991.

Levy, Jack S., *War in the Modern Great Power System, 1495–1975,* Lexington, KY: University Press of Kentucky, 1983.

Lewis, Kevin, "The Discipline Gap and Other Reasons for Humility and Realism in Defense Planning," in Paul K. Davis (ed.), *New Challenges for Defense Planning,* Santa Monica, CA: RAND, 1994.

Liska, George, *The Ways of Power,* Oxford: Basil Blackwell, 1990.

Lomperis, Timothy J., *From People's War to People's Rule: Insurgency, Intervention, and the Lessons of Vietnam,* Chapel Hill, NC: University of North Carolina Press, 1996.

Machlup, Fritz, *The Production and Distribution of Knowledge in the United States,* Princeton: Princeton University Press, 1972.

Mann, Michael, "The Autonomous Power of the State," *Archives Europeenes de Sociologie,* Vol. 25, No. 2, 1984.

March, James G., and Herbert A. Simon, *Organizations,* New York: John Wiley & Sons, 1958.

Marx, Karl, *A Contribution to the Critique of Political Economy,* 2d rev. ed., New York: The International Library Publishing Co., 1904.

Merritt, Richard L., and Dina A. Zinnes, "Alternative Indexes of National Power," in Richard J. Stoll and Michael D. Ward (eds.), *Power in World Politics,* Boulder: Lynne Rienner, 1989.

——— and ———, "Validity of Power Indices," *International Interactions,* Vol. 14, No. 2, 1988.

Migdal, Joel, *Strong Societies and Weak States: State-Society Relations and State Capabilities in the Third World,* Princeton: Princeton University Press, 1988.

Modelski, George, and William R. Thompson, *Seapower in Global Politics, 1494–1983,* Seattle: University of Washington Press, 1987.

——— and ———, *Leading Sectors and World Powers,* Columbia: University of South Carolina Press, 1996.

Molander, Roger C., et al., *Strategic Information Warfare: A New Face of War,* Santa Monica, CA: RAND, MR-661-OSD, 1996.

Morganstern, Oskar, et al., *Long Term Projections of Political and Military Power,* Cambridge: Ballinger, 1973.

Morgenthau, Hans, *Politics Among Nations,* 4th ed., New York: Alfred A. Knopf, 1967.

Murray, Williamson, and Mark Grimsley, "Introduction: On Strategy," in Williamson Murray, MacGregor Knox, and Alvin Bernstein (eds.), *The Making of Strategy: Rulers, States, and War,* Cambridge: Cambridge University Press, 1994.

Narin, Francis, *Evaluative Bibliometrics: The Use of Publications and Citations Analysis in the Evaluation of Scientific Activity,* Report to the National Science Foundation, March 1976.

Nettl, J. P., "The State as a Conceptual Variable," *World Politics,* 1968.

Nichiporuk, Brian, and Carl H. Builder, *Information Technologies and the Future of Land Warfare,* Santa Monica, CA: RAND, MR-560-A, 1995.

Office of the Under Secretary of Defense for Acquisition, *The Militarily Critical Technologies List,* Washington, D.C.: U.S. Government Printing Office, 1992.

Organisation for Economic Co-operation and Development (OECD), *Information Activities, Electronics and Telecommunication Technologies,* Paris: OECD, 1981.

Organski, A.F.K., *World Politics,* New York: Knopf, 1958.

——— and Jacek Kugler, *The War Ledger,* Chicago: University of Chicago Press, 1980.

Paret, Peter, "Military Power," *Journal of Military History,* Vol. 53, No. 3, July 1989.

Pavitt, K.L.R., *Technical Innovation and British Economic Performance,* London: Macmillan, 1980.

———, "Patent Statistics as Indicators of Innovative Activities: Possibilities and Problems," *Scientometrics,* Vol. 7, 1985.

Perry, William J., "Desert Storm and Deterrence," *Foreign Affairs,* Vol. 70, No. 4, 1991.

Popper, Steven W., Caroline S. Wagner, and Eric V. Larson, *New Forces at Work,* Santa Monica, CA: RAND, MR-1008-OSTP, 1998.

Porat, M., and M. Rubin, *The Information Economy: Development and Measurement,* Washington, D.C.: U.S. Government Printing Office, 1977.

Posen, Barry, *The Sources of Military Doctrine: France, Britain, and Germany Between the World Wars,* Ithaca: Cornell University Press, 1984.

Quah, Danny, *The Invisible Hand and the Weightless Economy,* Occasional Paper No. 12, London: LSE Center for Economic Performance, 1996.

Rasler, Karen, and William R. Thompson, *War and State Making: The Shaping of the Global Powers,* Boston: Unwin and Hyman, 1989.

Reed, John Shelton, "How Not to Measure What a University Does," *Chronicle of Higher Education,* Vol. 22, No. 12, 1981.

Ronfeldt, David, *Tribes, Institutions, Markets, Networks: A Framework About Societal Evolution,* Santa Monica, CA: RAND, P-7967, 1996.

Rose, Albert, "Wars, Innovations and Long Cycles," *American Economic Review,* Vol. 31, 1941.

Rosen, Stephen Peter, "Societies, Military Organizations, and the Revolution in Military Affairs: A Framework for Intelligence Collection and Analysis," unpublished manuscript, June 1996.

Rosen, Stephen Peter, "Military Effectiveness: Why Society Matters," *International Security,* Vol. 19, No. 4, Spring 1995.

———, *Societies and Military Power: India and Its Armies,* Ithaca: Cornell University Press, 1996.

———, *Winning the Next War,* Ithaca: Cornell University Press, 1991.

Rostow, Walt W., *The Stages of Economic Growth,* Austin: University of Texas Press, 1980.

———, *The World Economy,* Austin: University of Texas Press, 1980.

Rothwell, R. R., and W. Zegveld, *Industrial Innovation and Public Policy,* London: Frances Pinter, 1981.

Rueschemeyer, Dietrich, and Peter B. Evans, "The State and Economic Transformation," in Peter B. Evans, Dietrich Rueschemeyer, and Theda Skocpol (eds.), *Bringing the State Back In,* Cambridge: Cambridge University Press, 1985.

Rummel, Rudolph J., *The Dimensions of Nations,* Beverly Hills: Sage, 1972.

Russett, Bruce M., "Is There a Long-Run Trend Towards Concentration in the International System?" *Comparative Political Studies,* Vol. 1, 1968.

Schofield, S., "Defense Technology, Industrial Structure and Arms Conversion," in R. Coopey et al. (eds.), *Defense Science and Technology: Adjusting to Change,* Reading: Harwood, 1993.

Schultz, T., "Investment in Human Capital," *American Economic Review,* Vol. 51, March 1961.

Schumpeter, Joseph A., *The Theory of Economic Development,* Cambridge: Harvard University Press, 1934.

———, *Business Cycles,* New York: McGraw Hill, 1939.

Scott, W. R., *Organizations: Rational, Natural, and Open Systems,* 3d ed., New York: Prentice Hall, 1992.

Singer, J. David, et al., "Capability Distribution, Uncertainty, and Major-Power War," in Bruce Russett (ed.), *Peace, War and Numbers,* Beverly Hills: Sage, 1972.

Skocpol, Theda, "Bringing the State Back In: Strategies of Analysis in Current Research," in Peter B. Evans, Dietrich Rueschemeyer, and Theda Skocpol (eds.), *Bringing the State Back In,* Cambridge: Cambridge University Press, 1985.

———, *States and Social Revolutions: A Comparative Analysis of France, Russia, and China,* Cambridge: Cambridge University Press, 1979.

Snider, Lewis W., "Comparing the Strength of Nations: The Arab Gulf States and Political Change," *Comparative Politics,* July 1988.

———, "Identifying the Elements of State Power: Where Do We Begin?" *Comparative Political Studies,* Vol. 20, No. 3, October 1987.

Snyder, Jack, *The Ideology of the Offensive: Military Decisionmaking and the Disasters of 1914,* Ithaca: Cornell University Press, 1984.

Sprout, Harold, and Margaret Sprout, *Man-Milieu Relationship Hypotheses in the Context of International Politics,* Center For International Studies, Princeton University Research Monograph, Princeton: Princeton University Press, 1956.

Spykman, Nicholas, *America's Strategy in World Politics,* New York: Harcourt, Brace, 1942.

Sternberger, Dolf, "Legitimacy," in David L. Sills (gen. ed.), *International Encyclopedia of the Social Sciences,* Vol. 9, New York: Crowell Collier and Macmillan, 1968.

Stoneman, P., *The Economic Analysis of Technological Change,* New York: Oxford University Press, 1983.

Strange, Susan, "What Is Economic Power and Who Has It?" *International Journal,* Vol. 30, 1975.

Szafranski, Richard, "Peer Competitors, the RMA, and New Concepts: Some Questions," *Naval War College Review,* Vol. 49, No. 2, 1996.

Taber, Charles S., "Power Capability Indexes in the Third World," in Richard J. Stoll and Michael D. Ward (eds.), *Power in World Politics,* Boulder: Lynne Rienner, 1989.

Tellis, Ashley J., "The Drive to Domination: Towards a Pure Realist Theory of Politics," unpublished Ph.D. dissertation, The University of Chicago, 1994.

Tellis, Ashley J., Thomas S. Szayna, and James Winnefield, *Anticipating Ethnic Conflict,* Santa Monica, CA: RAND, MR-853-A, 1997.

Thompson, V. A., *Bureaucracy and Innovation,* University, AL: University of Alabama Press, 1969.

Thompson, William R., "Long Waves, Technological Innovation, and Relative Decline," *International Organization,* Vol. 44, No. 2, Spring 1990.

Tilly, Charles, "On the History of European State-Making," in Charles Tilly (ed.), *The Formation of National States in Europe,* Princeton: Princeton University Press, 1975.

———, "Reflections on the History of European State Making," in Charles Tilly (ed.), *The Formation of National States in Western Europe,* Princeton: Princeton University Press, 1975.

Toffler, Alvin, and Heidi Toffler, *War and Anti-War: Survival at the Dawn of the 21st Century,* Boston: Little, Brown and Company, 1993.

U.S. Department of Commerce, *Report of the National Critical Technologies Panel,* Springfield: National Technical Information Service, 1991.

van Creveld, Martin, *Technology and War,* New York: Free Press, 1989.

Walker, W., et al., "From Components to Integrated Systems: Technological Diversity and Interactions Between Military and Civilian Sectors," in P. Gummett and J. Reppy (eds.), *The Relation Between Military and Civilian Technologies,* Dordrecht: Kluwer Academic Publishers, 1988.

Waltz, Kenneth N., *Theory of International Politics,* Reading, MA: Addison-Wesley, 1979.

Wardynski, Casey, "The Labor Economics of Information Warfare," *Military Review,* Vol. 75, No. 3, May/June 1995.

Wayman, Frank, J. David Singer, and Gary Goertz, "Capabilities, Allocations, and Success in Militarized Disputes and Wars, 1816–1976," *International Studies Quarterly,* Vol. 27, 1983.

Weber, Max, *Basic Concepts in Sociology,* H. P. Secher (trans. and intro.), Secaucus, NJ.: Citadel Press, 1962.

———, *From Max Weber,* New York: Oxford University Press, 1946.

Woodall, Pam, "The World Economy: The Hitchhiker's Guide to Cybernomics," *The Economist,* September 28, 1996.

World Bank, *World Development Report 1992,* New York: Oxford University Press, 1993.

Wrong, Dennis H., *Power: Its Forms, Bases, and Uses,* New Brunswick: Transaction Publishers, 1995.

Zolberg, Aristide, "Strategic Interactions and the Formation of Modern States: France and England," *International Social Science Journal,* Vol. 32, No. 4, 1980.